Rituals and Practices with the
MOTHERPEACE
Tarot

Rituals and Practices with the
MOTHERPEACE
Tarot

VICKI NOBLE

Bear & Company
Rochester, Vermont

Bear & Company
One Park Street
Rochester, Vermont 05767
www.InnerTraditions.com

Bear & Company is a division of Inner Traditions International

Originally published under the title *Making Ritual with Motherpeace
Cards* by Three Rivers Press, a division of Crown Publishers, Inc.

LIBRARY OF CONGRESS CATALOGING-IN-PUBLICATION DATA
Noble, Vicki.
    Making ritual with Motherpeace cards : multicultural, woman-
centered practices for spiritual growth / by Vicki Noble.—1st ed.
    p.   cm.
        ISBN 0-609-80208-9 (pbk.)
        Includes bibliographical references.
        1. Tarot. 2. Spiritual life. I Title.
    BF1879.T2N56   1998
    133.3'2424—dc21

ISBN of current title : *Rituals and Practices with the Motherpeace Tarot*:
ISBN 1-59143-008-9

Printed and bound in the United States at Lake Book Manufacturing, Inc.

10   9   8   7   6   5   4   3   2   1

This book is dedicated to the Little People who showed up in such an active way asking to be manifested through the original Motherpeace images. May they continue to exist in the invisible dimension of our natural world, working away at their divinely elemental task of sustaining life on this dear planet. Blessed Be.

CONTENTS

ACKNOWLEDGMENTS

I am forever grateful to Karen Vogel for our original creative collaboration on the Motherpeace tarot cards back in the late 1970s, and for our ongoing and mutually rewarding friendship and business partnership since then. I've known Karen longer than almost anyone in my life, and she has participated actively in raising all three of my children. The Motherpeace images continue to inspire each of us to create new projects and make personal expressions that are informed by the same deep Mystery that transmitted itself through Motherpeace in the first place.

My heartfelt thanks to the Bogliasco Foundation for the fellowship I received, which allowed me to spend a month in Italy at the Liguria Study Center, where I was able to write the main body of this book. Besides providing me with near-perfect working conditions (my own studio, computer, supplies, E-mail, fax, wonderful staff and great Italian food!), the setting of the beautiful Villa dei Pini on the Italian Riviera, where I looked out at the Mediterranean Sea every day, was itself divinely inspiring. I felt blessed as I performed my private rituals on the balcony of my room overlooking the sea to be part of a long tradition of priestesses in the Old Religion of the Goddess that was so active for such a long time in that part of the world.

INTRODUCTION

This book is written specifically for women—those who use the Motherpeace tarot cards, and those who might not have heard of them yet. A revolution has taken place in America and Europe that has largely escaped the notice of the mainstream (male-dominated) media and academic institutions. The Women's Spirituality movement, started in the 1970s, has grown into a broad-based grassroots movement of "ordinary" women exploring the concept of a female-centered religious life, including ancient and modern images of the "feminine divine," in whose image we can begin to see ourselves as sacred. These women have shown a devout interest in opening their intuition, giving attention to their instinctual and body-based responses to life, and learning to fully embody the Shakti, or sacred female energies.

Since their first printing in 1981, the Motherpeace tarot cards have rippled out into the broader women's community in the United States and other countries, creating a small sensation in the area of tarot and the esoteric arts for women. Secretaries, social workers, teachers, therapists, and ministers are using them in their offices, schools, and corporations; luminaries like Gloria Steinem utilize Motherpeace cards as part of an eclectic spiritual path. Many traditional tarot decks designed by white men have alienated women because of their inherent sexist and racist assumptions and the negative attitudes that some of them expressed toward women. Like the women's movement that spawned it, Motherpeace is deliberately inclusive of diversity and purposely depicts people of color, older women, children, animals, and nonstereotypical images of men and women. Alice Walker, besides thanking us for making the cards in the introduction to one of her novels, tells stories about the cast doing Motherpeace readings between scenes while filming *The Color Purple.*

Since cocreating the Motherpeace images with Karen Vogel in the late 1970s, I have done thousands of readings with the cards, mostly for women and occasionally for men who want to know how to make better choices in their lives. I receive letters from Motherpeace users in places as far away as Japan, South Africa, Thailand, Australia, New Zealand, Mexico, Argentina, and Chile. A young woman in the Czech Republic recently wrote to thank me for sending her a deck of cards and a book, calling my attention to Prague's famous Black Madonna and the city's "amazing history of alchemists, magicians, and artists." Motherpeace functions worldwide as a shared visual "language of the Goddess" (to quote archaeologist Marija Gimbutas) that links women together globally across language and cultural barriers. I've frequently been invited by Catholic nuns to speak and teach at the different retreat and educational centers they direct, and I was once made an honorary "Sister of Notre Dame" at a California retreat.

Not long ago I received a letter from a woman notifying me about a friend incarcerated in a mental institution after being convicted of a minor crime. When the patient requested to have a deck of Motherpeace cards, her request was at first denied by the chaplain as "inappropriate" for her; Bibles naturally were permitted. I wrote a letter to the institution, suggesting that it was rather archaic of them at the end of the twentieth century to treat as heresy a deck of tarot cards so widely appreciated by modern women all over the world. They eventually released their prohibition and let her use the cards.

Using the cards to ask for an oracle (a process called divination) allows us to align ourselves and our actions with a larger cosmic order. In modern times, people question whether or not such a deep and sacred structure actually exists, but the practice of divination assumes, as Demetra George puts it, "belief in a Deity who is concerned with humanity and prepared to help."[1] For those of us in the women's spirituality movement, that deity is female, as ancient as her images from the Paleolithic (30,000 B.C.E.) and as benevolent as Tibetan Tara or Chinese Quan Yin, whose epithet is "She Who Hears the Cries of the World."

Demetra George and I have led groups of women on pilgrimages to Greece and Turkey. In her lectures to our groups, she has described natural divination as that which is intuitive, inspired, often takes the form of a visitation, and happens without an intermediary. In my writing over the years and in this book, I describe various occasions in my life when I have experienced such direct visitations and prophetic pronouncements.

Natural divination was part of ancient women's religion and was no doubt often experienced while in collective states of "frenzy" or the "orgiastic rituals" often mentioned in the classical Greek histories of Herodotus and Thucydides, among others. Through women's ancient shamanic practices, spontaneous prophecy or foretellings of collective events—such as the visions of Cassandra of Troy—came over women and forced them to speak the truth. This natural divination contrasts with the more formal responses in later times given by a priest or priestess (or nowadays a tarot reader) to a specific inquiry by a supplicant at a shrine or within the context of a ritual. Prophetesses (sybils, Bacchae, pythia, volvas, velas) in the earliest shrines experienced brief, abnormal states of mind in which they stepped outside themselves *(ecstasis)* through a divinely induced trance state while touched or filled with spirit *(enthusiasmos),* and they keened, sang, chanted, or otherwise poetically expressed their visions.

The most famous oracular center of this type was Delphi, where the Pythia gave her answers in a supposedly garbled form of speech that priests translated. At the height of its powers in the sixth century B.C.E., Delphi was the "omphalos" or oracular seat (the Pythia sat on a tripod) where everyone in the Mediterranean area came for guidance, both individual and governmental. Of the female sexuality implicit in the orgiastic trance state and its subsequent oracular speech, George points out that pythia were considered "brides of Apollo," just as Christian nuns are later described as "brides of Christ." And in this light, the second edition of *Webster's New International Dictionary* describes *nun* (from the Sanskrit *nana* or "mother") as a non-Christian "priestess or votaress."

It is impossible to adequately discuss the roots of natural divination without speaking of women's ecstatic religious practices, often described as Dionysian or Bacchic, and having to do with a complete abandonment of "ordinary" consciousness in favor of divine states of "possession" and "enrapturement." This "ritualized chaos or madness," as George so perfectly described it during our trips to visit ancient Greek oracular shrines, is expressed in the Greek word *manteia,* from which derive the words *mantic* and *mania; mainomai,* meaning madness; and *mantike,* which Cicero defined as "knowing the future." The inspired madness of these collective female ecstasies allowed whole communities of women (whom we know as maenads from the Greeks) to become filled with spirit in much the same way that contemporary Pentecostal women "speak in tongues."

We first hear about the maenads in Crete, although their antecedents are much earlier, to judge from Neolithic and Paleolithic cave images and wall murals. Figures of women dancing together in groups were etched on cave walls more than twenty thousand years ago, perhaps signifying the earliest recorded Bacchanalia. From Crete, however, we have written records of maenadic ecstasies. According to Carl Kerenyi, author of *Dionysos,* the maenads were "snake handlers," as one might suspect from looking at the famous Bronze Age Snake Priestesses from the palace at

Knossos, Crete, one of whom—wearing a high *polos* or head-dress—has snakes crawling up her dress, and the other—with a cat on her head—holds a writhing snake in each hand out to her sides. They were also "poppy eaters" (remember the *Odyssey*?), and in the Dionysian rites of their "cult" of Demeter, whose name in a Cretan script means "poppy fields," they intoxicated themselves with a potent herbal brew.

At Delphi we are told the priestess chewed on laurel and inhaled the vapors of the burning leaves in order to enter a violent trance state to answer the questions put to her. In Scandinavia the oracle was called *volva*, a prophetic woman wearing a headdress who sat on a high seat and pronounced on the past and future in a trance state that was understood to be facilitated from the Underworld or realm of the dead. The famous Voluspá or Sybil's Prophecy was pronounced by such a Viking prophetess as late as the eleventh century C.E. In Japan today, certain blind women act as "mediums," giving oracles in a trance state, and in Tibet the "mirror women" provide oracular prophecies.

Evidence demonstrates that oracles were originally part of a communal female process everywhere, probably connected to menstruation and the lunar cycles, and part of our early development as humans in social communities. The so-called psychic powers available to women during our collective menstrual periods would have been quite enhanced in the days before electric lighting and nuclear families, when women bled together as a group in tandem with the monthly cycles of the moon, such as the Native American Moon Lodge, which has survived into the 21st century. Ancient communal worship was organized around this magical female lunar cycle, as can be seen from the Paleolithic "Venus" figures and "calendar" bones discovered in cave sanctuaries where our earliest rituals were performed for tens of thousands of years. Microscopic analysis has shown that these early calendars were menstrual and lunar in nature; periodic cycles such as menstruation and pregnancy were most likely kept track of by shaman women for tribal purposes.

In later Neolithic (agricultural) societies, when people became settled in one place and grew the food they needed rather than traveling nomadically in order to hunt and gather it, the collective rituals of the female community must have become even more formalized and developed into the first organized "religion." Artifacts from Old European cultures of Vinca, Tripolye, Cucuteni in Eastern Europe; Sesklo and Dimini in ancient Greece; and Catalhöyük and Hacilar in Turkey provide consistent images of women in trance states, frequently in what we would now describe as yogic or meditation postures, and often with their mouths wide open, as if singing, chanting, or channeling some message of importance. Similar images of women are found in predynastic Egypt and in Mexico and South America at much later time periods.

From these images, we understand that "everywhere women were the original mantics," as Swedish scholar and painter Monica Sjöö stated in *The Great Cosmic Mother*. After the Neolithic period came the Bronze Age, with its invention of new techniques for working metal, which led to the weapons used in constant wars by patriarchal tribesmen who encroached on earlier peaceful cultures of the Goddess. But even during the Bronze Age, women retained the prophetic "office" all over the Mediterranean area (Turkey, Greece, Egypt, Malta, Crete, the Cycladic islands). Many of the figurines discovered at famous Bronze Age sites such as Troy, Ephesus, Delos, Delphi, and Crete portray women in trance, arms raised to "draw down" the power of the Moon, as Margo Adler put it in her book about modern pagans in America. Later, in the still more patriarchal and war-torn Iron Age, we find the familiar evidence of women acting as oracular priestesses, providing their communities with valuable information through oracular speech. An intact "frozen mummy" discovered in Siberia recently, preserved in ice from a burial mound of 400 B.C.E., was revealed to be a high-status woman wearing an extremely high headdress—so high that the woman wearing it required a wooden coffin eight feet long. Archaeologists believe she is part of this long tradition of priestess-women who gave oracles.[2]

But even though this ancient tradition of oracular women can be seen in evidence from all over the world and throughout all time periods, in our own modern culture we see very little demonstration of this powerful ability in women, especially in any sacred or religious context. Western women no longer practice going into trance states and giving oracles, nor are we normally asked by our government to do so![3] This noticeable absence of female participation in the religious and governing processes of our communities has been articulated by the modern feminist movement, and within that, the women's spirituality movement has focused on the development of female prophetic skills in particular.

In this context, Karen Vogel and I began to research and create the Motherpeace tarot cards in the late 1970s. We developed the cards, knowing that modern women need to reinvent our oracular skills and reclaim our prophetic powers. The Western world gives a passing nod to the validity of women's intuition but does not acknowledge it in any organized way. Women are assumed to know things but are more or less prohibited from acting on this knowledge. The ecofeminist movement attempts to articulate this "intuition" in the political sphere. We women "feel" the pain of the earth and "see" the catastrophic end of the world in sight, if humans don't act to change their behavior in relation to the environment very soon. However, the Western world historically has described women as "hysterics" and so today, as in the case of Cassandra of Troy, ignores our prophecies altogether.

But the prophecies insist on breaking through the cultural denial one way or another, and women seem to be the vessels of choice in every generation, regardless of whether or not there are cultural forms in place for channeling the oracular function of women.

A vivid example of this innate talent of women even in our modern technological society is the story of Charlotte King from Oregon, for whom the Charlotte Syndrome was named. In the late 1970s Charlotte King began to hear a tone, which at first she thought must be the result of a medical problem, and for which she sought treatment. But there was nothing physically wrong with her. She noted over time that the tone changed with the earth's movements. Although it seems unbelievable to our modern sensibility, Charlotte became able to predict earthquakes by the way in which the "tone" would change. Seismologists in the United States have corroborated her predictions and even relied on her for information at times. She has a Web site on the Internet and an emergency E-mail subscription, where her extremely accurate predictions of earthquakes and volcanoes can be found.[4]

I experienced a similar state of oracular precision leading up to the eruption of Mount Saint Helens in the spring of 1980. For six days I had been laid low with an extremely swollen and painful boil on my back, which my Motherpeace partner, Karen Vogel, had been doctoring with hot packs and tender loving care. On the sixth day, I told her that it "felt like a volcano that wanted to erupt." Unbeknownst to me, for exactly six days the mountain in nearby Oregon had been building up to its now-famous eruption. On the following day (May 20), when Mount Saint Helens erupted, so did my boil.

This experience transcended any philosophical stands I had previously held. Through this "inexplicable" but extremely physical experience, I was set free from whatever rational ideas had bound me up to that point. I understood in a wholistic way that "Her body is my body," as I later named a chapter in my book on healing, *Shakti Woman: Feeling Our Fire, Healing Our World.* We humans are part of Mother Earth in a way that goes beyond metaphor and reaches into the most tangible aspects of our lives.

CHAPTER ONE

TAROT AND WOMEN'S SPIRITUALITY

WHEN I FIRST TAUGHT MOTHERPEACE in the 1980s, it was seen as part of tarot, which was perceived as an "occult" art. Those interested in learning the tarot were students, and they delved into their studies about magic with an investigator's concentration, because they knew that the material was so esoteric, they would have to be serious in order to penetrate its abstruseness. The books I read in preparation for making our deck and writing my first book were obscure and written in a jargon that defied the normal use of modern English. The cards naturally were considered New Age, along with everything else "weird" to Americans, like channeling, using crystals, past-life regressions, and seances.

But, in fact, Motherpeace is not New Age and never has been. It has a feminist foundation and is absolutely grounded in shamanism and earth-based tribal healing practices. Motherpeace is a tool for modern women. The tarot community in America has never really found a comfortable place for these cards, which not only foretell the future but also boldly critique the present. The radical feminist challenge to modern society is to quit polluting, stop bowing down to the icons of white male privilege and elitism, and think again about the models we want to use to measure ourselves. "Motherpeace" is literally that—a model of the peaceful lifestyle that issued from millennia of worship of the Great Mother, and the highly evolved organization of society around her ancient principles of cooperation, relatedness, egalitarianism, and ecstatic communion.

Motherpeace was designed with the female oracular talent in mind. The images of the Motherpeace deck are taken from ancient cultures and contemporary tribal peoples to remind ourselves at this late date in Western history that we are not alone here. The Motherpeace images are predominantly female (previously unheard of for a tarot deck, except for another round deck of tarot cards called Daughters of the Moon Tarot; the women who created this deck lived in Northern California and were creating the images at the same time that Karen and I were making the Motherpeace cards in Berkeley during the late 1970s), multicultural and multiracial, varied in age, with lots of animals and plants to signify and enhance our connection to nature. Many of the images portray women in "oracular" kinds of activities, that is, in touch with the invisible dimension and receiving information from there.

For example, in the suit of Wands, women are shown with flames coming out of their mouths (7 Wands), having a vision (2 Wands), creating spontaneous rock art (3 Wands), celebrating an initiatory transition such as the menarche or "first blood" (4 Wands), meditating in profound trance (9 Wands), and celebrating an orgiastic rite in which an adolescent girl speaks in tongues while a scribe writes down what she says in ciphers on a circular clay tablet (10 Wands).

Wands

Or in the suit of Cups, women dance an ancient magical circle dance with snakes, as was done in Crete (3 Cups), a woman waits for the oracular dove or "holy spirit" to descend into the silver cup on her head (7 Cups), women dance and sing at a wishing well, a sacred spring, or perhaps a mountain shrine like Karphi in Crete, where they are overseen by a Cretan Poppy Goddess with upraised arms (9 Cups), and a whole community of Anasazi or "ancient ones" raises their arms in gratitude and collective worship at a site like Chaco Canyon in the American Southwest (10 Cups).

Cups

In the suit of Discs, the oracular activities may not be as obvious, because they are not as direct, taking place as they do on the "earth" or physical plane. But even so, the 7 of Discs shows a pregnant woman in a calm state of waiting, a condition that may include visions and provide information; the 8 of Discs shows several women at work on various crafts, and it is known that the act of weaving and spinning can cause an altered state of consciousness in the weavers, so oracles are sometimes woven into "storycloths" for a newborn child; 9 of Discs shows a solitary, creative medicine woman at work on a sand painting, an activity that is also understood to produce altered states and otherworldly communication; and 10 Discs shows a woman giving birth at home, supported by midwives, in the company of a circle of women who are all no doubt in trance or unusual states of mind resulting from the presence of the kundalini energy known to accompany natural birthing.

Discs

Similarly, the suit of Swords may not have as many images of strictly oracular women, but some can be inferred from the various activities shown on the cards. The Ace of Swords, for instance, shows a woman in yogic meditation with "second sight" enclosed in a clear crystal; 2 Swords shows a woman balancing in the Stork posture and "gazing" or engaging in Taoist meditation; and 4

Swords depicts a woman inside a pyramid in a deep meditation state, the colors of her seven chakras or energy centers clearly portrayed behind her spine. The 6 of Swords shows six women flying above a forest with their swords touching at the center of a mandala. This is interesting when you remember that in the Middle Ages women in Europe were being burned at the stake for the crime of being "witches," which included the accusation of flying through the woods at night. Scholars have shown that pagan, shamanistic people (particularly the women) at that time used to cover themselves with "flying ointments" made of powerful psychotropic herbs, which allowed them to "journey" out of their physical bodies into other realms, as shamans have always done in every land. Even the 9 of Swords, which shows a nightmare vision of phantasms and frightening apparitions, could be a "bad trip" on hallucinogenic plants that qualifies as oracular and perhaps warns of some hideous future prediction.

Swords

Many of the so-called People cards also depict oracular consciousness at work in the lives of different ancient or tribal peoples around the world. For instance, the Daughter of Discs is standing in a stone circle at the top of a mountain with a cave in the background; she is holding an obsidian mirror up to receive impressions from the rising full moon and the setting sun, just as other ancient people have done throughout the millennia. The Priestess of Discs is practicing yogic asanas on her antelope rug, and we see the vision she is having in the mandala to one side of her, with two dragons winding around the open eye in the hand of the "seer."

The Son of Cups, enclosed as he is by the egg that reminds us he belongs to the Mother or the "feminine," is held in a state of bliss brought on by the consumption of the sacred datura flower pictured at the base of the image. Some scholars think the datura could be a part of the ancient Soma drink of the ancient Indian rishis, and a similar image of a sacred male in a yogic meditation pose comes from the pre-Aryan Goddess-worshipping Indus Valley culture of the area that is now modern Pakistan. The Priestess of Cups is a mermaid in telepathic contact with the whale shown in the water below her, as well as in mystical communion with the snake-haired Full Moon in the twilight sky. And the Shaman of Cups is masked in white gypsum (or chalk), which was used by ancient priestesses around the Mediterranean for rituals and has been found in the graves of Amazon priestesses as far east as Russia and Central Asia.

The Daughter of Wands runs and leaps in the tradition of those shamans from the northern lands who ate the *Amanita muscaria* mushroom, which produces enhanced physical strength and boundless energies for the sacred work of healing. (The same mushrooms are depicted in the Fool card in the Major Arcana—the twenty-two Roman numeraled cards in the deck.) The Son of Wands, painted all over and dancing in the tradition of the "sacred clown," has entered a trance state through the medium of communal dancing and drumming. The Priestess of Wands carries an ancient Paleolithic baton de commandement (carved bone staff) and is accompanied by the lizard of transformational healing; her eyes blaze with consciousness of the beyond.

The Daughter of Swords is whistling for the North Wind in the tradition of the Amazons, whose graves contained ritual bone whistles and fabulous horse trappings. The Priestess of Swords, with her ceremonial axe of authority, is shown as the archetypal seer, looking into the night sky as she communes with the owl of wisdom with its ancient oracular power. And the Shaman of Swords, taking her cues from the kite, an oracular bird, practices the widespread ancient divinatory form of augury, or taking omens from bird flight. She could be a Sauromatian warrior priestess–queen of the Russian steppes in 600 B.C.E., commanding her people with the force of her truthful, passionate insights.

Just by virtue of the images themselves, then, the Motherpeace cards function as role models for modern women who might be having some of these strange (by our standards) experiences of the female oracular voice. Just as Charlotte King and I began to "feel" (and embody!) the earth changes taking place in the early 1980s, so many modern women are seeing and feeling similar changes both in their bodies and through their psychic experiences. A whole network has developed for helping people having so-called spiritual emergencies, spontaneous and often violent awakenings of psychospiritual powers and forces that cause them undue hardship and pain, even madness, if they have to fend for themselves without support from or contact with others who have gone before them.[5]

Using the Motherpeace cards has proven to be a saving grace for women who might otherwise be terribly afraid of the sometimes frightening visions and spontaneous events taking place in their lives. A woman who sees herself in one of the pictures feels less isolated and alone in her "weird" experiences. And simply because the cards are physical or material and are held in the hands, they calm and ground the person using them. Just shuffling the cards can be an exercise in tranquility and centering, which most of us need desperately in our fast-paced modern lives. Astrologers and psychics predicted that the Aquarian Age would bring us a "heightened vibration" and an "accelerated" process of change, and now, with the entry of its ruling planet, Uranus, into the sign of Aquarius in the spring of 1995, these prophecies are coming true. We all feel things speeding up these days, especially with the Internet and other global communications networks.

It is entirely possible to use the Motherpeace cards without any instruction, and without any knowledge of the system of tarot or its ancient oracular tradition. Simply having a deck—perhaps keeping it on an altar or near your bed—and picking it up now and then, shuffling, and looking at the pictures is enough to make a woman feel safer and more at ease in her own spiritual process. Letting the feelings and sensations in the body guide and provide information is one good way to begin using the cards. Remember that just being born a woman gives you an oracular edge! And if in addition you pay attention to the cycles of the moon and your own menstruation, and you use the cards at those powerful times when the moon is new or full, your experience will no doubt be amplified by those natural conditions, which tend to open the psychic "eye" and allow for insight, expanded knowledge, and the ability to see into past, present, and future in the tradition of our ancient foremothers in every culture.

YOUR FIRST ORACLE: STARTING TO READ THE MOTHERPEACE CARDS

For your first experience with the cards, why not choose a single Motherpeace card and spend time looking at the picture. You might like to set the ritual scene a bit, with candles or incense burning, quiet or meditative music in the background, a special scarf or altar cloth on which you lay your cards. To begin, just shuffle or mix the cards in any fashion you like, and then at random, with the deck of cards facing down, choose one for yourself in this moment. I like to pour the whole deck out into a circle (facedown) and then choose a card without thinking about it. Several people at once can do this together, in a women's circle or a group of friends.

Spend some time just really looking at the image. Take in all the details and symbolism. Notice how you feel, and especially any sensations or impressions you register. I always like to remind women that those things we tend to push aside are often where the real information resides. For example, if you choose a card and immediately like or dislike it intensely, this is not to be ignored but rather to be incorporated—it's part of your information! Any "charge" from the card is telling you something about the content, as well as what it might mean in your life. So pay attention to everything at once and simultaneously see if you can empty your mind of the usual judgments and critical thoughts. Keep it playful.

Notice the colors and textures, the energy, the action and story, in the picture. What is the age, race, sex, of any people? Are there animals, plants, stones, artifacts, and other objects that give you hints about the meaning? Anything familiar to you from your own studies or lifework will have a special "oracular" meaning. Sometimes the cards are quite literal, for instance giving the 7 of Discs to a pregnant woman, or the 3 of Discs to a builder.

Discs

Discs

But mostly the cards are working at a metaphorical level, showing you an imaginative story or narrative that somehow carries over or applies to your life in the here and now. If you read the card in the following two stages, you will most easily succeed at the reading:

first, you tell the story (the action in the picture), and then you make a wild guess about how it applies to your life.

Once you feel comfortable doing this kind of reading for yourself, try it on a friend. It's often easier to read the cards for someone else, because your own "stuff" is not in the way. Have your friend pull a card and make an exchange with her. Read the picture then guess what it might have to do with her life at the moment. It's especially fun to do this before you and your friend check in with each other, so that you can try your metaphoric skills at being a card reader. Share with each other after you have read the cards, giving feedback and corroboration. You might like to have a partner in your work to exchange with on a regular basis.

I was interested to learn that the Norse volvas (the Scandinavian priestesses who gave the oracles) functioned professionally in groups of nine, traveling and working together. You might decide to gather a small group of women friends together who are interested in learning to work with the Motherpeace deck. Together you can explore and encourage one another in your studies, taking some of the isolation out of your "esoteric" work.

CHAPTER TWO

FATE AND PERSONAL WILL

PEOPLE HESITATE TO PICK UP A TAROT
deck or get an astrology reading on account of the false idea that
using them means turning over your free will to a predetermined
future. The whole idea of fate seems highly misunderstood in our
scientifically based Western world, where we are convinced we can
(and should) control everything, from our bodies to the workings
of nature herself. Contemporary New Age philosophies haven't
helped much, with their blatantly elitist ideas expressed in simplistic slogans such as "You create your own reality." This could seem
plausible if they are just talking about the affluent leisure class of
New Age yuppies living in Northern California, but it is ludicrous
when referring to starving Ethiopians or North Koreans. Any reading of the complex workings of fate needs to be broad enough to
apply to everyone.

For those unfamiliar with the mystical significance of numbers, it may seem surprising that our understanding of fate could

be so well illustrated by the number three, whose sacred meaning was profoundly understood by our ancestors. The number three has a natural rhythm of birth, life, and death; beginnings, middles, and endings. It's a way of describing everything as energy that's always moving, ever changing. Everything is understood to be coming in, staying awhile, and going out of manifestation. Three Fates are found in the mythologies of many cultures. Contemporary High Priestess Zsusana Budapest has written a great new book on the workings of the Fates in European tradition.[6] In Norse mythology, the three Norns were the Fates who lived under the Yggdrasil, or the Tree of Fate (depicted in the Motherpeace Justice card), sharing similar characteristics with the earlier Greek Moirai, also a threesome: Clotho, the spinner; Lachesis, the one who measured the thread; and Atropos, the one who cut it.

VIII

Justice

This natural system personifies the human understanding that our birth, life, and death are in some respects already assumed or known, written in the book of fate as it were. Within that profound structure, we have choices and exercise our individual free will.

Real life for most of us does seem to be a mix of at times being able to control or manipulate reality while at other times being seemingly at the whim of forces beyond our control, and we try somehow to station ourselves in the middle of these paradoxical possibilities and find a balance. In ancient times, there was a shared understanding about the workings of natural law. The Fates were perceived as divine female beings whose interventions were for the larger good of the whole. Oracles were perceived as messages from the Fates and were utilized as a means of aligning oneself with the deeper or revealed truth of the patterns and rhythms underlying outer events, thereby helping humans to make decisions that would be in our best overall interest. If you got out of balance with what nature had in mind for you, then it was understood that the forces of fate would set things back in place. As uncomfortable as that might be for individuals, it was acceptable because of its value for the group or for the planet. Modern people have stopped using oracular means to determine which direction to go, what decisions to make, and generally how to stay in balance or harmony with the larger world in which we participate.

ANCIENT GODDESS CULTURES AND FATE

Ancient cultures of the Great Mother developed the creative arts and crafts such as pottery, basketry, spinning, and weaving. The Great Mother herself was connected both to the fecund Earth (fertility and growth) and the constantly changing Moon (ecstasy and rebirth). This Double Goddess ruled day and night and was portrayed not only as a birth giver and nurturer, but as the Death Goddess and "weaver of fate." In a famous Mexican sculpture, the Mayan Moon Goddess Ix Chel is shown sitting at her loom, weaving the fates of all the living. Women especially honor Ix Chel, who also rules pregnancy and birth, and until very recently her islands off the coast of Yucatán were still places of pilgrimage for Mayan women, who still understood that the souls of those to be born were under the protection of the Fate Goddess. Spanish chroniclers on ships accidentally blown off course in 1511 described seeing on one of these islands large statues of goddesses dressed in flowers and facing out to sea, and they saw women wearing gold and finely embroidered costumes doing ceremonies; they named it Isla de las Mujeres or the "island of women."

Life and death were not held as separate entities by ancient people, who consistently portrayed the Goddess as both giver and taker of life. "We all come from the Goddess, and to her we shall return like a drop of rain flowing to the ocean," goes a chant written by Z. Budapest and sung in women's spirituality groups around the world. The earliest religion embodied both realms, and the oldest "cemeteries" were usually places of community ritual. In Malta, the underground hypogeum, which housed the remains of seven thousand inhabitants of that island interred over the course of more than a thousand years, was also an awesome ritual temple of mystery and ceremony carved by hand from limestone with Stone Age tools made of antler bone. The "oracle room" is an underground chamber with a carved hole through which, when a person sings or vocalizes, the sound can be heard throughout the entire three-story structure.

A famous figurine called the *Sleeping Lady of Malta* found in the hypogeum illustrates the deep connection to fate felt by the ancient Maltese. Dressed in the typical pleated skirt seen on other priestess or Goddess statues found on the island of Malta, she's lying on a bed on her right side with her arm resting under her head. Tibetans who practice "dream yoga" suggest you "lie on your right side like a lion doth," and archaeologists think the *Sleeping Lady* may represent a kind of dream "incubation" that was practiced in this ancient womb-tomb. She could also represent a pregnant woman sleeping in the temple for the purpose of incarnating into her womb a spirit of the ancestors buried there, a ritual that is in the tradition of some African peoples, as Malta is less than two hundred miles from the coast of Africa. The earliest recorded understanding of the Fates is this profound acceptance of birth, life, and death as a continuous flow of energy through forms.

In County Sligo, on the northwest corner of Ireland, from the same time period (fifth to fourth millennium B.C.E.) there are Neolithic "cemeteries" where remains of early people were interred under stones arranged in circles, piled up in cairns, or balanced in dolmens. As in the Maltese hypogeum, active community rituals were performed here as well. Ancient people constantly acknowledged through the Fates the connection of the living and the dead. On a nearby mountaintop overlooking the most famous of these cemeteries, Carrowmore, with its beautiful variety of stone structures laid out over the land, is the famous burial mound of the Queen of Fairy (depicted on the Motherpeace Strength card).

Strength

There is a portent of fate connected with this sacred place: the practice of carrying a stone to the top of the mound and making a wish on Queen Maeve's Cairn is a link to pilgrimage sites on mountains named for goddesses everywhere in the world.

In later periods (Bronze Age, Iron Age) the oral tradition of the Mother Goddess was put down in writing, and we have narratives and mythologies describing the workings of natural law and fate in her world. The classical Greek goddess Themis or Egyptian Maat represents the fundamental underpinnings of oracle and prophecy, which articulates a deep structure known as "natural law" or justice.

It is this deep invisible structure that holds our material world in place and provides the understood context for oracular warnings or predictions. All oracular pronouncements are designed to help people take responsibility for making right choices that are in keeping with these "natural laws," or to help people understand the "consequences" that accrue from any breach of these deep prevailing patterns in nature. This invisible structure underlying the physical world allows us to use something like the tarot cards; it's what makes them "work."

THE THREE-PART STRUCTURE OF THE MOTHERPEACE CARDS

Over the years I have developed a form of working with the Motherpeace cards that helps integrate this paradox of fate and free will in our daily lives. The fundamental three-part structure of the system of tarot is the basis of this formula, so that when working with the system I've developed, you also study and learn the tarot at a deeper level than you might otherwise. To use this system, you'll need to divide your deck into the magical three piles of cards: twenty-two Major Arcana (with Roman numerals and titles), sixteen People cards (Daughters, Sons, Priestesses, and Shamans in each of four suits), and forty numbered cards or Minor Arcana (ace to 10 in each of four suits).

VII

Chariot

Shaman

Discs

7

Wands

Put the three stacks in front of you facedown: Majors on the left, People cards in the middle, and Minors on the right. You're going to ask three questions, and the answers will be found by drawing one card at "random" from each of the three stacks and laying that card faceup in front of you. When you are ready to begin the reading, you will be looking at three cards in a row—a Major Arcanum, a People card, and a Minor or numbered card.

The best frame of mind for beginning with the cards is to suspend the normal "critical mind," with all of its scientific beliefs and judgments, and try to begin from a place of neutrality. Act "as if" the cards will work, even if you feel skeptical. The questions you ask the cards in order to formulate a narrative that will become your reading are directly related to the whole issue of fate and free will. In a simple sense, the Major Arcana, known as the "big cards" in the deck, carry the most weight and represent the workings of karma or fate. The People cards in the middle represent your personality or soul, which is attempting to deal with the forces and archetypal powers that are at work in your life. The numbered cards have to do with the arena or realm of your life where the incoming force or fate is likely to show itself or materialize.

The Majors represent forces much larger than our individual egos and therefore things we are unlikely to be able to change or affect on our own. This is where you learn to let go, to "trust the universe" or "go with the flow," and to try and align with something bigger or higher than your own ego structure. You can't change the situation represented by the Major Arcana cards. The personal work indicated here involves getting out of the way— trying not to resist the events and happenings in your life—rather than flailing at the universe or forcing your will where things don't seem to be working. It can be a comfort to know that there is something larger than the individual. To really begin to know that we are "held," and to live life from that understanding, is a profoundly important part of the Goddess religion or any other bona fide spiritual path.

The People cards are an interesting area in between fate and personal free will. As images of ourselves, they represent the integrated personality in the world. Daughters and Sons cards represent younger parts of the self, and Priestesses and Shamans are older, more mature expressions of our individuality. The People cards represent a situation that is somewhat mutable but not easy to change. For example, if you don't like the card you chose and the style of expression that it describes in you, or if the card is upside down, indicating a difficulty, you can change yourself through deliberate intervention such as long-term therapy, body work, or other means of transforming the personality. It isn't easy and it takes time, but it can be done.

Finally the numbered cards (ace through 10) in the four suits (Discs, Cups, Wands, and Swords) tell you the area of manifestation, the place or sphere in which the whole situation will resolve itself or come to completion. Discs represent earth energy or the physical plane; Cups water or the emotional realm; Wands energy and the realm of the passions; and Swords air and the intellectual world of ideas. Discs usually indicate the body, money, work, or physical activity of some kind; Cups show dreams, desires, feelings, and psychic experiences such as telepathy; Wands show communication, warmth, sexual excitement, and vitality; and Swords indicate thoughts, perceptions, insights, and what is seen with the physical eye. The realm of Discs can be sensual or rigid, Cups pleasurable or melancholic, Wands intuitive or overwrought, and Swords can indicate either clarity or struggle.

The Minor Arcana, and particularly the numbered suit cards, are the least binding and the most transitory of all the cards in the deck. In a person's regular life she may not be reflecting on cause and effect, so there is an "inevitability" about any outcome from the causes that set the process in motion. This inevitability is represented by the future position in any past-present-future reading format. But with consciousness, some potential situations can be changed, and these changeable conditions are represented by the Minor Arcana. Certain situations depicted by these numbered cards can be diverted in a moment by skillful mental focus. If you don't like the card you draw from this third pile, just wake up— pick another one! You aren't stuck with anything in this realm; this is absolutely the area of life in which you truly can create (or at least renegotiate) your own reality. A "bad card" might indicate nothing more than a passing mood, a momentary anger, a temporary fear or anxiety, a fleeting but probably habitual negative thought. Whether you stay in this negative space is up to you; you have the power to change it by changing your mind, altering your mood, transforming your energy, or letting go of the temporary feeling. The Minor Arcana teach us about mutability and fluidity, personal responsibility and free will.

In my classes I often teach women how to transform their situations through the use of shamanic tools such as a rattle or smudge, herbs such as sage or cedar burned to cleanse a space. These physical objects have an observable power to change our brain waves and therefore alter our experience immediately. If, for example, you wake up one day in a bad mood, you can choose to stay that way if you wish, allowing it to intrude into your day and bear negative fruits, such as ill will, angry flare-ups with people around you, or just being on a general bummer. But if you pick up a rattle and shake it for as few as five minutes, I guarantee that you will not be able to stay in the same negative state, because the sound of the rattle will break through your inertia and literally and physically change your bad mood. The same phenomenon is true if you burn sage, sweet grass, or some other good-smelling herb that cleanses and purifies the space around you. Or you could beat out a rhythm on a drum, say a mantra, or sing a chant. The transformation is irresistible and empowering, and it can be repeated as often as needed.

THE FATE READING

So now that you are ready to do your fate reading, the questions to ask are:

1. What is the archetypal or "big force" at work in my life at this time?
2. How am I "channeling" or working with this force, that is, how am I handling or managing it as it moves through my life?
3. Where in my life is it likely to "manifest" or take shape, that is, in what realm am I likely to be able to see it?

You select the three cards and begin to meditate on them, one at a time. First spend some time with the Major Arcanum, sinking into it with your psyche, letting yourself merge with the image on the card. Imagine the Fates at work in your life, intervening in your unconscious process to set things right, applying pressure toward some alignment with natural law, perhaps even shattering or dissolving patterns and habits that have defined your identity up to now. Your current situation, which is reflected in the Major Arcanum, is a result of past forces, choices, and events that were set in motion in the past and are coming to fruition in the present moment. Although it is not usually possible to alter the overall situation indicated by the card, you can melt your defenses and open yourself to the impressions and guidance that may be available along with the energies represented. As always when working with the Motherpeace cards, you want to use all of your senses, allowing your intuition, as well as your feelings and thoughts, to be a part of the reading. Put yourself in the picture and see what that brings up for you.

Then move on to the second card in the reading, the People card, this character in the middle who most closely resembles you. Can you imagine yourself as the person depicted in the card? How are you like this? In what way is the picture describing your situation? Use the image to tell a story that involves action and drama, and enliven the story with your imagination: Who is this person? What is she (or he) doing? Feeling? Thinking? Saying? Where is she going? Why? How does it apply to you, to your life, your participation in work, home, family, community, or world? Who are you in terms of the elements in the card? All the People cards have two elements represented by the suit (Discs = earth, Cups = water, Wands = fire, Swords = air) and the title (Shaman = fire, Priestess = water, Son = air, Daughter = earth).

Finally take a look at the third card in the formula, the card from the small or minor suit. From the suit you can figure out immediately on which plane of existence this situation or event is taking place. Discs indicates the real world, whereas Cups suggests the dream realm of feelings and emotions. Wands tells you the situation is energetic rather than concrete, and Swords suggests there could be trouble. The whole realm of earth energy (Discs) is slower and takes longer to effect changes, whereas in your dreams (Cups) things can change much faster. The world of fire (Wands) is the volatile realm of passions and anger, and in the airy realms of the mind (Swords) things change at the drop of a hat. Once you've determined the element and how that feels or impresses your imagination, then just "read" the picture, letting the story of the activities depicted become a metaphor to describe your present situation.

The tricky part of this formula or "reading layout" is to put it all together into a coherent narrative or story that becomes your fate reading for the day or week or year. You can put any time period on it as a structure, but obviously you should decide on it before you choose the cards and lay out the reading, for it will determine how much weight the cards carry. A birthday reading or a reading done on the New Year will be stronger and the effects of it last longer than one done every day or every week. One way is not better or worse than another, and there are no rules about how much or how often you can use this formula.

MOTHERPEACE STUDY PLAN: A YEAR AND A DAY

For the purpose of learning the Motherpeace cards in a way that encourages a deep, structural understanding of the whole deck, I would suggest the following use of this reading format. Keep your regular deck of cards available for other kinds of readings and for playing with friends, working with clients, carrying with you in your purse, and so forth. Get a second deck of Motherpeace cards that you can keep in three stacks all the time on an altar or some special place where you can come to it on a regular basis, preferably every day. Decide on a plan of study that fits your daily schedule. If you can't come to the deck every day, because your life is too busy or scattered, then you will have to choose a regular pattern of study (for example, Saturday mornings) that makes sense given the truth of your situation.

I suggest that you study the cards for "a year and a day," in the traditional initiation period of the Old Religion of the Goddess. You begin with a ritual of entering, and you end with a celebration or initiation ritual. These can be spontaneous and impromptu rituals that are designed by you in intuitive and simple ways. Or if you're up for a more elaborate process, you can begin by making promises or vows to keep your practice or discipline, and end with some sort of test, feat of courage, or celebration, such as having a "graduation" party and doing readings for your friends, or having a business card made so you can start to do readings professionally for clients at the end of your specified year.

So every morning (or at whatever interval you have established for yourself) you choose a card from each of the three stacks and do a short reading for yourself. It might help to write down your thoughts and intuitions, although it is not necessary. The important thing is that you attempt to "prophesy" what the reading is telling you about the day (or week or month) that it covers. Then you go through your day and return to your altar that night before bed to look at the reading again. This is the crucial step. You look at the reading from the perspective of having lived through your day, so in retrospect you will have more information than you had when you were more or less guessing what the reading might mean. From your lived experience, you know exactly what each card was referring to. Now you have embodied the reading, and the meaning of the cards will be forever inside of you as a starting point when you read for yourself or others.

As you go through this initiatory period of a year and a day of study, you can also take in as much information as you like from books and teachers, adding to what you are learning from your intuition and your own experience. You can't really have too much information, as long as you make your own impressions the starting point. Among the texts you choose, you might want to work with *Motherpeace: A Way to the Goddess,* the book I wrote that goes into great detail about the symbolism of every card, including its historical, mythological, and archaeological background, and my suggestions about what it might mean in a reading. At some point in your course of study, you may want to use the *Motherpeace Tarot Playbook,* with its in-depth esoteric systems of using the cards, including reversed meanings and a variety of complex reading layouts, as well as astrological correlations to the Motherpeace deck. Karen Vogel has recently come out with a small Motherpeace book focused on divination, which you may also want to incorporate into your perspective.[7]

When I had a school for healers in Oakland for four years during the end of the 1980s, I had my students keep a journal with two columns, one on the right for how they were taking responsibility for "free will" in their daily lives, and one on the left for how they were surrendering to "fate." As part of your year of study, you might like to keep some kind of similar record of the way you are able to learn to recognize the difference between fate and free will, when one or the other is called for, and how you are doing in your process of learning to find a balance between the two. Most people lean in one direction or the other—too passive (it's all fate) or too controlling (it's all up to me)—and the process of observation and self-awareness that comes from this ongoing regular practice of the fate reading in your daily life can be very illuminating.

CHAPTER THREE

SHIFTING
WITH FATE
(MAJOR ARCANA)

IN THE LAST CHAPTER, I DISCUSSED the difference between fate and free will and offered a reading layout for learning how to find a balance between the two. In this chapter I will go more deeply into the Major Arcana cards themselves and make suggestions on how you might handle the powerful influx of fateful forces and energies into your life. We are at a notable disadvantage in the West in regard to the so-called big energies because we cling to a rigid sense of our personal identities and our beliefs about the world. Historically Christianity has demonized the dark, invisible forces that earlier generations of Europeans took for granted, while scientific materialism denied that they existed. Westerners—and especially Americans—are the only culture in the world that denies the presence of the "little people" or fairies, the intelligent consciousness of plants and animals, and the vibrations of the planets and stars.

Through our cultural denial of such invisible, magical forces, we have habitually contracted our invisible energy bodies (often called auras) until they fit inside our physical bodies, isolating us and making it seem as if we are smaller than we are. Although our energy bodies are linked with our physical bodies, esoteric teachings tell us that they have the capacity to extend out from our physical bodies into the space around us, and ultimately to receive impressions from anywhere on the planet out into the universe, as well as engaging in interspecies communication. In the rock art and cave paintings of our ancestors on every continent, it would seem that these extended energy bodies were part of every culture's shamanistic or sacred worldview. Early traditions suggest that out-of-body experiences were common, and "shaman flight" was practiced by individuals for healing as well as collectively in ecstatic religious rites.

In order to effectively handle the incoming transformational energies of certain Major Arcana, such as the Tower or the Death card, it helps to stretch ourselves and become more flexible—psychically, emotionally, and mentally—so that the changes that want to happen can take place with the least disturbance on the physical plane. Otherwise every transformative experience will be linked with bodily difficulties, such as accidents or illness, and outer-world shatterings (for example, losing your job, your mate, your house, and so on).

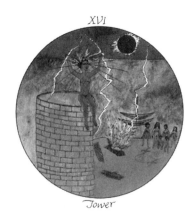

Tower

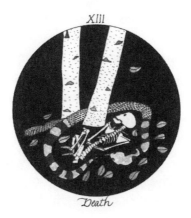

Death

There is a way to "dance" with the energies and forces, but it takes practice and a fluid sense of identity. If the ego has congealed around a fixed or rigid sense of itself—that is, if you identify with or have become permanently wedded to who you *think* you are— then you will experience an "ego death," which may be quite uncomfortable, even debilitating.

Sometimes women are one step ahead in this process of spiritual development, because development of women's ego identities has in part been thwarted by Western culture, and there isn't such a rigid identity to let go of. But by the same token, it takes a strong sense of self in order to be fearless before the powers and energies of the invisible world. Often the process for women on the spiritual path involves on the one hand developing a creative ego, and on the other, letting go of ego patterns. You need to feel anchored to something solid or certain, something that is really there, in order to be able to let go *into* something. For those of us in Women's Spirituality, that something is the Goddess or the deep structure of the Mother, which we have learned to trust to safely hold us. When we let go of the enormous effort of holding ourselves together, we find that there is a safety net in the deeper psychic structure into which we have anchored ourselves through ritual.[8] This is the structure of natural law ruled by the Fates.

In my classes, I have often suggested to my women students that they make an effort to identify with the snake and its magical ability to shed its skin. The snake is the female totem par excellence, and figurines of women who are part snake exist from the Neolithic period and later in various parts of the world. These snake women help us to understand in a metaphoric way women's special ability to change and transform, which is connected with the lunar cycles and our periodic menstruation. Think about it. Every month for much of our lives, we women bleed and shed our (inner) skins, the lining of the uterus. In shamanism it is necessary to practice or rehearse death, in order to become proficient at moving from one dimension to another at will. Shamans are the experts at going into trance and journeying out of the body to other realms, and by having their periods, women spontaneously practice this feat every month with regularity.[9]

The snake is also the symbol of spiritual energy, known as kundalini, which is pictured in yoga as a coiled snake resting at the base of the spine, waiting to be awakened through spiritual practices. However, this kundalini energy is spontaneously catalyzed every month during the bleeding time, creating a strong psychic experience for many women, even though we may not have known what to do with it! Over the course of a woman's life, there are many opportunities for such spontaneous awakenings of the kundalini energy, which is believed in India to belong naturally to women. The kundalini itself is often depicted or discussed as being a great snake who is a goddess, and when awakened, "she" rises up your spine through your chakras or energy centers, bringing cosmic consciousness and supernatural powers called *siddhis*. One of the most likely contexts for the awakening of "kundalini-Shakti"—the creative fire—is through the act of natural birth, which any midwife will attest to. Unfortunately, in America women rarely give birth in a natural way at home anymore, thus losing one sure channel for raising the kundalini energy and attaining spiritual wisdom.[10]

MAJOR ARCANA: KUNDALINI-SNAKE
THROUGH THE CHAKRAS

One way of perceiving the powers represented by the Major Arcana is to think of them as depicting the various states one might experience as the kundalini snake rises up through the seven chakras, stimulating and awakening consciousness as she goes.[11]

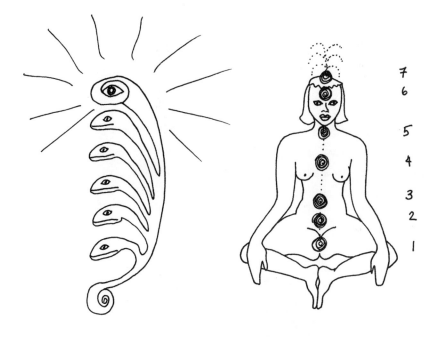

THE FOOL represents the entire realm of possibility, the pure impulse or open window of psychic experience, the precise formless moment of awakening before the energy has taken any shape. The feeling here is one of enormous freedom and spontaneity, as if anything might happen. It's very childlike and open, completely free from fear, trusting the universe and moving with the flow of energy or power.

Fool

THE MAGICIAN is the spontaneous fire, Shakti, the heat that heals, the awakening of power, assertion, passion, and drive. It's as if something has lit your *root chakra* pilot light and anything can be done, any intention mobilized, any dream manifested. This is the original "can do" energy, the first spark that makes things happen, moving the body into action. When somebody says, "Just do it!" they are describing the Magician. You go, Girl!

Magician

THE HIGH PRIESTESS is related to the *second chakra* and the awakening of the nighttime, psychic powers and inner, visionary capacities. This is the doorway to heaven and the possibility of using

Tantric or sacred sexuality as a route to the highest spiritual states. Unconscious psychic abilities become manifest in this energy center—telepathy, clairsentience, and extrasensory perception—and an extraordinary dream life awakens. Keep a dream journal.

High Priestess

THE EMPRESS represents the integration of what esotericism calls "life in the three worlds," the physical, emotional, and mental realms. Here is the archetypal woman—mother, creative artist, fertile field. She holds the key to the active intelligence in the world, the *third chakra* of personal power and individual identity, and the ability to bring into manifestation whatever is needed to support life. She connects, nurtures, engages, relates, and creates. Make art.

Empress

THE EMPEROR is like the Magician—a manifestor—but he is particularly concerned with the making of culture. The *fourth chakra* is home to the Soul, with its task of balancing between the higher and lower centers, and the Emperor represents the force or power it takes for the soul "on its own plane" to determine reality in the physical dimension. But you need to be disciplined and focused to build forms and create structures. Get bossy.

Emperor

THE HIEROPHANT, originally the patriarchal voice of authority, becomes the awakened inner voice and ability to hear your spirit guides. As the kundalini snake rises to this level and opens the *fifth chakra*, the birth of "female authority" can take place. This center is very intuitive. Speak your mind.

Hierophant

THE LOVERS depicts the enormous conflicts we experience between the sex-role stereotypes we have been given and the innate sense of wholeness we feel at the center of ourselves. When the kundalini snake rises to the level of the *sixth chakra,* we glimpse reality clearly as it is. We integrate the paradoxes, bring together the opposites, unify the polarities. Your third eye opens.

Lovers

THE CHARIOT represents a warrior-priestess queen, the unified human being working from the spirit center *(crown chakra),* through all the energy centers, and then into the world. The Amazon driving the chariot has the ability to protect herself while remaining open, and to get things accomplished in the world while staying in touch with invisible realities. Throw an oracle!

Chariot

THE JUSTICE shows a new level of awareness in the *root chakra*, an attunement to the workings of karma and natural law. Now in addition to simply having personal energy for making things happen, there is an urge to align with nature, to work for social justice, to participate in bringing peace on earth. Join Earth First or the Sierra Club.

Justice

THE CRONE represents Vesta, the original temple priestess in her wisdom aspect of Wise Old Woman. As Persephone turned into Hecate, the Crone's Queen of the Underworld, the dead, and the night, awakening the *second chakra* to owllike wisdom and Sybilline dreamtime prophecies. Her sexuality has been contained and mastered and is part of her ancient "virginal" autonomy, which is harnessed into a higher purpose. Practice yoga.

Crone

THE WHEEL OF FORTUNE lights up the *third chakra* with gifts and rewards of earlier manifesting activities. An astrological transit changes your identity, and as the wheel turns, you become someone new whom you've invented through deliberate actions in the past. Your power expands as you receive what you deserve. Take a new name.

Wheel of Fortune

THE STRENGTH CARD depicts a new level of power in your *fourth chakra* ability to order reality and "bend" energy to your will. From the deepest level of your heart-mind, you put your healing will to work in the world from the invisible realms of the ancient ones. Utilizing the helping forces and power animals from the "other" side, you can transform the world the way you wish. Cast a spell.

Strength

THE HANGED ONE shows the method of surrender to your sacred calling as shaman, healer, priestess, minister, mother, teacher, artist, or leader. The how-to is in the letting go, learning to trust the higher power that speaks through your inner ear *(fifth chakra)* and manifests your destiny. There is no longer room for any resistance. Follow your bliss.

XII

Hanged One

THE DEATH CARD demonstrates the impermanence of all forms, and the fluidity of the energy that enlivens them. What you see with your third eye *(sixth chakra)* is that nothing dies yet everything changes. Old forms are discarded as regularly as leaves falling from the tree, the snake shedding its skin, or the light changing with the seasons of the year. Grieve, and honor your changes.

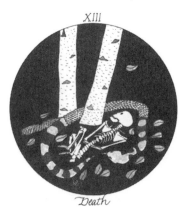

XIII

Death

THE TEMPERANCE represents the second level of mastery reached at the *crown chakra* when an alchemical process of transformation has been completed. Now the Amazon—master of the physical plane—becomes the creative artist balanced between the extremes of the psychic and emotional worlds, managing the enormous incoming powers without losing her footing. Do a ritual.

Temperance

THE DEVIL shows us the problems that are likely to arise once we have tasted the powers and abilities borrowed from the invisible world. The *first chakra* urge to power makes itself felt in materialism, "cockiness," and physical greed, the temptation to make it at someone else's expense, and to inflate the ego by amassing money or physical strength. Break an addiction.

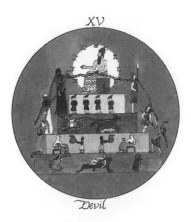

Devil

THE TOWER represents the shattering force of transformation, a *dakini's* unpredictable lightning bolt of change. Dakinis are Tibetan female tricksters and transformational goddesses, similar to the Indian goddess Kali. This high-vibrational energy can be channeled if you are willing, but it takes courage and the physical groundedness that comes from knowing, through yoga practice or martial arts, how to move the kundalini energy. You have to center yourself in the *hara* or womb center *(second chakra)* and let the energies move through you like an empty vessel, without attachment. Fasten your seat belt, and let her rip.

XVI

Tower

THE STAR depicts the integrated ego in the calm after the storm of transformation or enlightenment. The high-vibrational energies are received and transmitted through the expanded vessel of the body, which has become an instrument of healing. The identity *(third chakra)*, cleansed of its habitual attachments through the now-continuous influx of change, is flexible enough to resemble Changing Woman. Make a prayer.

XVII

Star

THE MOON shows us that the illuminated soul has now to turn itself over to the dark night once more, making its spiral way through the labyrinth of the unknown in order to reach a new level of awareness and ability to heal *(fourth chakra)*. The pull of the instincts is the only sign that lights the way to mastery, and the outcome is as uncertain as any throw of the oracle. Make a trance journey.

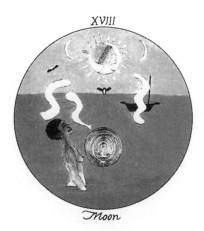

XVIII

Moon

THE SUN is the breakthrough, the rebirth, the much-appreciated arrival of spring after a hard winter. The heart sings and the *throat chakra* opens with gratitude, creativity, and joyous self-expression. Miraculously the fears and doubts that have plagued the personality in the past are released, and the simply human appreciation of each moment becomes available. Celebrate.

Sun

THE JUDGEMENT marks a transformation recognized, that moment when consciousness moves to a new level of awareness, and you know that your soul has made a decision that will affect your future through all time. The eye of compassion *(sixth chakra)* is opened, the "rainbow bridge" is crossed, the invincible "diamond body" is built. Heal yourself.

Judgement

THE WORLD is the final level of integration of spirit in matter, the Goddess in the world, the divine in nature. Now you know who you are—all your past lives can flow into this one, all your selves be brought exquisitely into a form that expresses your wholeness. This is the intelligence of the awakened *crown chakra* acting through the human body-mind on the physical earthly plane. Be yourself.

RITUALIZING MAJOR ARCANA LIFECARDS

In my *Playbook,* I have discussed in detail lifecards and how they are calculated from the numerology of your date of birth. Here I will briefly reiterate the method of calculation, and then I will discuss the transitions from one year to another ("year cards") and how you might create personal rituals for yourself to help with those incoming new energies for each new year. The lifecards are portrayed by the Major Arcana, so my discussion will be based on the images in the cards and their archetypal connotations.

To calculate your "soul" and "personality" or lifecards, you add your birth numbers in a column, then add the sum sideways (horizontally) until you arrive at number 22 or less. For instance my birthday is April 13, 1947, so I add the numbers in a column and arrive at the sum of 1964:

$$4$$
$$13$$
$$\underline{+\ 1947}$$
$$1964$$

Then I add the sum horizontally to get my two cards: 1 + 9 + 6 + 4 = 20 (XX Judgement), but since it has two digits, I add again to get a single digit: 2 + 0 = 2 (II High Priestess). Someone else might get 21 (XXI World), which "reduces" (2 + 1) to 3 (III Empress), or 18 (XVIII Moon) reducing to 9 (IX Crone). In most cases, there are two numbers, the higher one (in my case 20) representing the "personality" and the lower one (for me two) the "soul." But a person's birth numbers could add up to the sum of 1975, which when reduced, or added horizontally (1 + 9 + 7 + 5), equals 22. Since there is no Major Arcanum numbered "22," the zero (0 Fool) is arbitrarily substituted for it; then 22 is reduced by adding again horizontally (2 + 2 = 4) to arrive at IV (the Emperor) and 0 (the Fool) as the person's life cards. Another case might culminate in a sum that reduces to 23 (2 + 3 = 5 Hierophant) or 24 (2 + 4 = 6 Lovers), and so on, providing instead of two lifecards only one, which represents both the "soul" and the "personality." Then there is the spectacular case of the number 19 (XIX Sun), which when you add it sideways equals X (Wheel of Fortune), which is still a double-digit number that must be added again to get I (Magician). In this case the middle number is treated as a "wild card" while the higher one is the "personality" and the lower one the "soul," as in the rest of the cases.

Sometimes the first number reached will be greater than 22, so there will only be one Major to represent both "soul" and "personality." For instance, there is no Major Arcanum with the number 23, so that number (and others higher) must be reduced to its single-digit counterpart, which is 5. The V (Hierophant) serves as both "soul" and "personality" card. And one other slight exception is the number 22 itself, which is not used on any Major Arcanum and must be replaced with 0 (Fool) for the "personality" and reduced to IV (Emperor) for the "soul" card.

To calculate the "year cards" use exactly the same process, but instead of the birth year, you add the current year to your day and month of birth, then reduce the sum by adding the numbers sideways. Whatever Major Arcanum number you get for the year, you stop with that, rather than reducing to the single digit. So, for example, if your numbers add up to 27, since there is no Major with that number, you have to reduce by adding them together and getting IX (Crone) as your year card. If the numbers add up to 20, which is a Major Arcanum, then you keep that number as your "year" card and work with XX (Judgement) rather than reducing to II (High Priestess).

Once you figure out this system, you can use it to determine any year of your life. And if you want to follow the years in sequence, you can interpret what the different "year cards" have meant in your life. In Mary Greer's book on the lifecards, *Tarot Constellations,* she provides a graph that is very useful for seeing the overall pattern created by the changing lifecards. For our purposes, it will be enough for you to determine last year's card, this year's card, and next year's card. Sometimes they go in order, and sometimes the order breaks, so don't assume a constant sequence. You won't know until you calculate them from your own birthday numbers for the current three-year period.

"YEAR CARD" READING LAYOUT USING THE MAJOR ARCANA

Once you have calculated your current three years, find the three Major Arcana that correspond to them and lay the three cards out in front of you from left to right, or from past to present to future. You have already lived through last year, so work with that image for a while until you have a sense of what it's telling you as an oracle. Hopefully last year's image will give you a fresh sense of meaning about the overall year and some of the experiences or teachings it contained. Sometimes the synchronicity as seen in retrospect is quite striking. Then spend some time with the middle card for the current year, and see if it makes sense as an indicator of what you have been going through so far. In the card for any year, you will be able to determine the tests and challenges put to you in that year, as well as the energies and forces needed to pass those tests and conquer the challenges.

Finally you are ready to do the "divinatory" work of looking into the future. Concentrate on the third card, the one on the right that represents the coming year. Try to really feel or "drop" into the image and imagine yourself in it. Study it for hints and intuitions of what the year might be bringing for you. The new energy begins to make an influx into your life at the changing of the numerical year, around January 1. But I generally begin to feel it anytime after the Winter Solstice, at the end of the current year. Pay special attention during that time to the kinds of events that emerge, and the feelings and impulses you find yourself having. Winter Solstice and the New Year signify the time when the "seed" is planted for the year—whatever is going to materialize during the coming year has its first incipient moment at the beginning of the year. The energy ruling the year then takes root or "manifests" concretely around the time of your birthday, whenever that happens in the course of the year. For some people this means a very short period between the beginning of the influx and the taking hold of it; for others, with late birthdays, it means a longer period in between.

MAKING RITUAL

Generally speaking, it would be a good idea to ritualize the beginning of each year in some way, to celebrate and acknowledge the entry of this new energy into your life for the year. The New Year is a natural time for ritual. I always like to throw some kind of oracle on New Year's Eve to see what the next year holds for me and my loved ones. Including your awareness of the "year cards" adds depth and personalizes your New Year's ritual. The content of the ritual will vary according to the archetype of the "year card" about to begin. The following suggestions are to catalyze your thinking about ritualizing the new influx of energy. Use them as jumping-off points for yourself, and create your own intuitive rituals for you to share with your family and friends.

0 (FOOL) for the year indicates that you would want to do something playful or wild; honoring the Fool would be to welcome in the "inner child" and break form in some way; consciously do something different.

I (MAGICIAN) might mean you would work fire into your ritual, acknowledging the power of the candle flame, the spark, or the burning away of the past so that something new can begin.

II (HIGH PRIESTESS) might suggest using a mirror or a bowl of water in your ritual for gazing into the future, or to find the still voice within, it might suggest going to an ocean or a river, or doing quiet meditation.

III (EMPRESS) could mean you should get out in nature and feel the earth, hug a tree, take a walk, or plant a rosebush. You could cook a fine dinner, have a massage, create art, or make a baby.

IV (EMPEROR) means you're going to need to be really focused this year in order to make things happen in the world of form. Perhaps you will want to get a résumé together, or make an outline for the new project you want to complete during the year.

V (HIEROPHANT) shows that the issue for you this year is your spiritual authority. You might decide to write your own prayer or liturgy, start your own women's circle, become a therapist, or join an existing religious organization of some kind that meets your specific spiritual needs.

VI (LOVERS) suggests that relationship is going to be on your mind this year. You might wish to make a list of the qualities you want in a partner and tuck it into a "medicine bag" until spring. An already existing relationship might require some special attention; perhaps a sacred ritual lovemaking session with your partner is in order.

VII (CHARIOT) indicates that the task for you this year is to become more independent and autonomous. You might want to do a ritual of cord cutting that frees you psychically from any dependencies you've established. You might create a wand or staff to symbolize your "central axis" and sovereignty over yourself.

VIII (JUSTICE) is the card of karma and promises that you will get what you deserve as things come into harmony and right relationship. You might throw the *I Ching* to determine what it is the Fates have in store for you in this coming year.

IX (CRONE) suggests a year of isolation, introspection, and listening for guidance. You could take a day or two over the New Year to go on a solitary retreat, withdrawing from the usual New Year's Eve madness into a more monastic setting where you can hear your inner voice.

X (WHEEL OF FORTUNE) is a time for getting it out there, so perhaps you will want to send work off to a publisher, or make plans for an exciting trip somewhere during the year. Jupiter rules the year, so make strong wishes, since they might come true!

XI (STRENGTH) brings in the profound magic of the shaman-witch, so gather natural materials you find outdoors (bones, feathers, sticks, stones), plus old beads and things you've saved over the years, and make a "fetish" to welcome the coming year. Put your agendas out to the universe.

XII (HANGED ONE) usually asks you to let go or sacrifice something you thought you wanted, in favor of something different that your higher self chooses. Make an offering of all your disappointments by holding a rock and letting the rock absorb your sorrow; then sacrifice it at your altar, or in the woods, or at the ocean, and don't look back.

XIII (DEATH) means endings, finality, something's over. Go to a cemetery and meditate on your life up to this point—take stock, get current. Then clean out your closets and throw away everything obsolete and outdated. Make way for the new.

XIV (TEMPERANCE) ushers in a new experience of power in balance, finding the mean between the extremes. Get art supplies and make something of beauty, without judging your talent. It's the process that counts. Walk a tightrope or a balance beam.

XV (DEVIL) brings a heavy energy, the hard work of facing your addictions and overcoming them. Gather together photos of your family of origin, plus current photos of yourself and your close relationships, and sit with them long enough to begin to see negative patterns that you might be able to cut through during the coming year. Start therapy.

XVI (TOWER) indicates shocking, possibly catastrophic change, so prepare yourself by laying some groundwork: find someone in the helping or healing professions that you can call on to hold your hand as you go through the year. Take up karate.

XVII (STAR) seems to imply a gentle year of grace, recovery, and healing. Light a candle and take a long, hot bath with sweet-smelling herbs or bath salts. Give thanks for all that you have endured, and let the light of high-voltage healing into your cells.

XVIII (MOON) brings a new challenge, a profound initiation into new and unfamiliar territory. Stand in front of a mirror and look at yourself until it puts you into trance, and see how your face changes. Ask yourself over and over, who am I?

XIX (SUN) means a happy-go-lucky year full of life energy and not much stress. Take a child to the zoo or a park and play on the climbing gym. Go to Disneyland. Sign up for a class in something frivolous you've always wanted to learn but never had time for.

XX (JUDGEMENT) is transformation and healing, a spiritual elevation or revelation, what they used to call "the judgment day." Make a cup of mugwort (Artemisia) or saffron tea and drink it before bed to stimulate a "big dream." Get a brand-new dream journal and initiate it.

XXI (WORLD) is the work completed; the breakthrough to new consciousness; becoming your total self. Make a collage of photos of yourself from different times in your life, especially those that show visible changes. Arrange them in a pie shape showing your various "incarnations," with your current self at the center of the circle.

CHAPTER FOUR

FORTUNE-TELLING (PAST, PRESENT, AND FUTURE)

IT'S AMAZING HOW MUCH FEAR COMES up for many people at the idea of "telling the future" or even "knowing the past." As a culture, we're almost completely out of contact with our own active sixth sense, that paranormal part of our consciousness already in touch with everything. However, even now, in most places where such practices are technically considered heresy or backward superstition, women still practice methods passed down from their foremothers. When I was in Turkey a few years ago, I met a bright young woman while I was looking at kilims (flat-woven tribal rugs) in her brother's shop. I read the Motherpeace cards for her in exchange for her reading my coffee grounds in the tradition passed down to her by her grandmother. She was having her period, which meant that she was forbidden by the Islamic religion during that time to pray in the mosque; but there were no such restrictions on her reading the sacred coffee grounds.

To understand how it is possible for someone to look into the past or see into the future, we need to give up the concept of linear time. Esoteric wisdom teaches that past, present, and future are no more than constructs thinly overlaid on reality by our human minds, and that, in fact, everything is happening at the same time. There is something about the possibility of falling into this *real* time that frightens us; we feel safer with things organized in a neat, linear way. This kind of rational order to Western thinking, which originated during the classical Greek times, hit its apex during the so-called Enlightenment in the Age of Reason and continues to influence us today. However if everything is happening at the same time, then we have access to the terrifying reality of the Burning Times (when enormous numbers of so-called irrational women—healers, ritualists, herbalists, and midwives from the old pagan traditions—were burned at the stake in Europe for the crime of being "witches") right this minute alongside our everyday contemporary reality and along with the reality of ancient Goddess cultures. That subtle undercurrent of memory or psychic experience is enough to make us ambivalent about delving into the "occult." The fact that organized religions today still actively demonize the practices and principles of the old pagan religion of the Goddess only adds to our anxiety, while the resurgence of Women's Spirituality brings us closer to the time when pagan religions were the dominant cultural force.

In early twentieth-century Ireland, we are told that everyone, even Catholic priests, still participated in rituals and practices concerning the "wee people" or "faery folk." The prehistoric mounds in Ireland that tourists visit today, such as New Grange and Knowth, were understood to be the abodes of the Elfin Queen and her people, who (according to the stories) can capture or seduce humans into their realms, where time becomes irrelevant, no one ages, and every wish is fulfilled. In this way, the Irish acknowledge the two dimensions—visible and invisible, past and present, non-material and physical—that are interwoven into what we call "reality." Marion Zimmer Bradley's enormously popular *Mists of Avalon* played on this theme of the disappearance of the Old Religion into the "mists" of time and behind the "veil" of material reality, where it still exists to this day.

One of the central understandings of the old ways was "reincarnation," or the sense that we have each been alive on the planet many times—hundreds or even thousands of times—and that these "past lives" can bleed into the present one, providing both the nourishment of information and guidance as well as the confusion of inexplicable compulsions and phobias. It is no accident that modern Western people don't believe in reincarnation today and that we act as if it is a superstition left from archaic times. The development of our rational paradigm took many centuries and included many specific steps in the erasure and negation of the old concepts and understandings. Reincarnation was declared to be a Christian heresy and was explicitly banned at the beginning of the fourth century of the Common Era, when the Council of Nicea proclaimed that there was no such thing as cyclic reality. From that time on, there were severe punishments (including death) for any behaviors or activities that revolved around such a heretical belief.

I have written in other places about my own direct experiences of reincarnation and past lives.[12] When you have an encounter with the past, or a direct experience of past, present, and future coexisting at once, you are popped out of the Western linear paradigm whether you like it or not, and immersed in the revealed truth of direct perception. This direct perception is related to the High Priestess card in the tarot, the open window of the intuitive mind, the nighttime consciousness of the dreamtime. Such revelations of truth are undebatable, since they transcend the normal sense of belief or nonbelief. You have simply experienced the reality of it for yourself, and therefore you know.

I had a spontaneous and blissful out-of-body experience on Candlemas Eve, February 1 (one of the four sacred "cross-quarter days" of the Goddess religion; see chapter 8), and I heard a voice say, "I am one with all witches through all time." This experience changed my worldview. I then discovered that Candlemas is traditionally the day of Witches' Initiation. The integration in my conscious mind of this powerful synchronicity catalyzed an even deeper level of revelation in my psyche and unlocked the "doors of perception," which allowed profound visionary experiences to occur. It is from this seed vision that my entire destiny has unfolded.

Now, twenty years later, my dreams are consistently precognitive, and I frequently experience the overlapping realities of the invisible world with this precious physical world that we erroneously call ordinary or mundane. I have become accustomed to knowing things in advance, and I am comfortable in my vocational identity as a seer. My interpretations are not always correct, but I can truly say that at this point, I dream almost everything of importance a couple of months before it happens. When I'm away from home, I dream about my children and loved ones, connecting (sometimes quite literally) with their lived experiences from an unfathomable distance. For me, these experiences across time and space provide a feeling of safety and make me feel secure, and I know I am held in the loving arms of the universal Mother.

When I use the Motherpeace cards to look at the past, interpret the present, and intuit the future, I am using the skills developed through more than twenty years of daily practice. All spiritual practices are designed to be repeated daily until breakthroughs happen and pinnacles of psychic awareness or spiritual consciousness are reached. When you begin doing readings to look at the past and imagine the future, you must remember that it takes practice and perseverance to get good at it. Don't expect in the first reading to see correctly into future time. Be patient and give yourself opportunities to make mistakes and learn from the cards themselves about how to read them. On the other hand, don't be surprised if one day when you least expect it, you have a direct perception of the "other dimension."

READING PAST, PRESENT, AND FUTURE WITH THE MOTHERPEACE CARDS

For this reading, you will use the entire deck of cards. It's important to set the tone of your reading by being in a meditative space—perhaps burn a candle or incense first—and grounding and centering yourself in some way. If you don't have a "centering" practice, try sitting quietly with the deck of cards in your hands, and imagine a root growing from your spine down through the floor and into the earth. Once you can "feel" the root connecting with the earth, then imagine your spine growing up from that root like the stem of a plant, and your head growing up from the stem like a flower, open to taking in "light" as nourishment, just the way a plant would. In this way, you open your *root* and *crown chakras* for healing power and information to flow through you.

Mix and shuffle the cards in any way you like, and when you are ready, pull three cards from anywhere in the deck and place them faceup in the order drawn, representing past, present, and future. Now sit for a while and let the cards speak to you through their colors and forms. Don't try to think about what they mean, or worry over what they are trying to tell you. Just let them sink into your psyche, giving you information through all the channels that are open to you. When you feel ready, begin to "read" the card representing the past, by telling the story of what you see in the image. Describe to yourself (or a friend) the persons, plants, or animals in the image, the activities they are involved in, the feelings and thoughts you are having in relation to the image, and finally what you think it refers to in your recent past. This last part is the intuitive leap you always make from the story told in the cards to the prediction made by the reader.

Sometimes when you read the pictures in the cards, you will be drawn to specific places in the image, which is not necessarily the "most important" place according to your rational mind. Go wherever your consciousness feels drawn and begin to tell a story. Even if you are attracted to an apparently trivial part of the picture, let yourself dwell on it until it unfolds through narrative, trusting that the information you are getting is worthwhile and will lead you somewhere. For instance, in a card like the Priestess of Wands, it may not be the Priestess herself who attracts your attention in a particular reading but the lion beside her, or even the cauldron way in the back of the picture, or the rainbow, or the lizard. Just go where your intelligence is drawn and follow through with the reading. In this way, you will activate your intuition and spark psychic powers, and your natural reading abilities will be awakened.

It's easiest to begin with the card representing the past because you can corroborate it with the information you have about the present. You have already lived through the past, so you can confidently figure out what the image in the card is pointing to. No doubt you will be given deeper insights as well and make some links that help you to integrate and assimilate past experiences, and sometimes the card in the past position will provide a "missing link" to help you reframe your present experience by thinking in a new or healthier way about what has recently happened to you. This is how the visionary consciousness opens into the past.

Psychics even tell us we can heal the past. By calling it up in our memories, we can "go back" into it with our imaginative faculties and change it, and by doing this kind of intervention, we can then effectively transform our experience of the present. If we really do want to "create our own reality" in any meaningful sense, it is actually necessary to do this work on the past. So when you work with the card in the past position, even though you have already "been there, done that," don't assume anything, and don't be too certain that you understand everything it's trying to tell you. There is always a deeper level of information available in any reading, if you are willing to go there.

The card in the present position relies heavily on what has happened in the past. In certain ways, it shows only the inevitable unfolding of the momentum arising from whatever has been set in motion from past events and actions. A thorough understanding and acceptance of the past, with all the responsibilities and awareness thereby included, is necessary for a complete reading of the present. Let yourself look into the present with visionary eyes and not take it for granted just because you are "in" it right now. There are levels, and then levels, of potential awareness at any given moment, and most of the time we are using much less of our faculties than is actually available to us. See if you can meditate on the card in the present position and sink into a deeper level of "seeing" it.

Once you have slowed yourself down enough to really look at the card, begin to put yourself into it in an imaginative way. If there is a central character, see if you can "become" her or him for a moment. What does it feel like to be this person, or this animal, or this archetype? Go deeper. Who are you in this context? What do you *know*, by becoming this person or being? If the card is a Minor Arcanum—one of the more "mundane" cards—you may not feel you can become very immersed in it. The 2 of Discs may be no more than a direct reminder to you about your immediate juggling act, describing how you are trying to work on a project and take care of a child at the same time, and the to-be-expected difficulties of such an undertaking. On the other hand, perhaps a deeper reading of the card will take you into an unexpected contemplation on the two-headed snake or the Celtic wheels, and then to the metaphoric level of the film reels and the daily drama of your life. Maybe the energy of the crescent moon will begin to affect you in some way. You might experience yourself in meditation as a breast-feeding mother of twins, which could have an emotional component you hadn't expected. The point is to give yourself over to the images with your imaginative consciousness, and let your reflection on the card become a kind of journey.

Once you have entered into the reading on this level, you will have a more profound sense of what has transpired recently and how you got to where you are at the moment. Your feelings, thoughts, anxieties, hopes, and dreams will be clearer, and you may have achieved a kind of momentary precious detachment, which the Buddhists speak about when they teach meditation practices. You may have the capacity to be in your life experience and also to "witness" it at the same time. This witnessing consciousness is the part of you that is most likely to be able to read the future without the normal resistance or blockages that come from your ego-fears.

Sometimes the result of getting in touch with your reality on this level is that you become more truthful with yourself, allowing the whole picture to come into focus. You can see the karmic seeds that led to this moment, having observed that point in the past when you set in motion the events that have naturally unfolded to become the now that you are presently experiencing. In this way, it is possible to take full responsibility for what is happening in your life, without judging yourself or blaming someone else for the consequences you are currently experiencing. Moments of seeing the whole are like states of grace, and they allow a profound integration to occur in your psyche. Take advantage of the moment and inhale deeply, relaxing and actually allowing a natural forgiveness to arise in you with the breath.

Now riding on that wave of truth, you can look at the card in the future and it will be neither frightening nor surprising. The future arises directly out of the present, which unfolded logically from the past, and it's all happening in this single moment in time. According to esoteric tradition, we have all the information available to us all the time; we just don't use it. And as a conscious being with free will, there is a good possibility you will be able to affect your future experience in a meaningful way, if you are able to encounter it consciously. So look at the card and see how you feel about it. Notice your reactions without trying to get rid of them.

The future is what you have to look forward to, so your reactions and feelings about it are crucial to your moving healthfully from present to future time. If you feel afraid of what's out there, or if it turns you off, then you want to be able to hold or contain those feelings in the present moment, rather than going into denial. This holding is one of the deeper teachings of meditation and contemplation. Can you tolerate your experience without running from it? Can you just be with yourself as you directly confront reality? By distracting ourselves with some outside stimuli we have been trained to flee from any experience we find uncomfortable. This is partly why Westerners are more or less always in motion and rarely at rest, except perhaps when we sleep.

The Vietnamese Buddhist teacher Thich Nhat Han advises naming your present moment in order to help you learn to stay in it. For instance, if the reading so far has brought sad feelings into your consciousness, you might say to yourself something simple, such as, "I am feeling sad, lonely, angry, depressed, frustrated," or whatever it is that you have gotten in touch with through the past and present cards. Rather than brushing off the experience and rushing on to the next one, you hold yourself in present time by simply naming your experience, your situation. This ability to hold yourself in present time is very powerful and can lead to intense spiritual healing.

Then in the momentary equilibrium of the felt present moment, you can allow into your field of consciousness the picture of what can be expected in your future. If the card in the future position is a Minor Arcanum or People Card, it's only a possibility anyway and not binding. You can assess it and see whether or not you want to go there, and if you don't, you might be able to make an intervention that will negate it or at least alter it somewhat. This is what the "science of divination" was based on in classical times. People would ask the oracle about the future, and if it was "negative," the oracle would suggest certain ritual actions they could perform to appease the spirits thought to be responsible for the predicted occurrence, thereby changing the outcome.

Let's say as an example that your future card is the 7 of Swords, showing a fox stealthily approaching a chicken coop where swords are lined up on a fence like a ladder. In other words, you are all set to enter into a strategic mental activity, where you will be trying desperately—with your mind (Swords)—to figure out a way to get something that you think you need to be crafty about getting.

Or if you identify with the chickens, then you are likely to put yourself in the position of a victim, passively worried about something "bad" happening to you that you can't avoid. Either way, there's a lot of tension and anxiety, all based on some idea of scarcity.

Swords

A lot of the Sword cards describe or depict mental situations brought on by fear or doubt, which then grow into moments filled with the struggle of anxiety, compulsion, phobia, and the intense planning that we hope might stave off the inevitable "bad" situation we are dreaming up and reacting to. This compulsive activity of the mind is what Buddhists describe as monkey mind, and it creates a lot of unnecessary stress in our daily lives. So what can you do? In the process-oriented psychology of Arnold Mindell, one suggestion is to "change channels" in order to find a more effective way to handle your experience. Changing channels pops you out of your habitual, unconscious tendencies and into the fresher, more open space of being able to make a new decision. Somehow you have to stop thinking about the problem and do something else.

So with 7 Swords, perhaps you could try an exercise I give my clients when they feel afraid or anxious about something "bad" that could happen in the future. When a fear arises in your mind, the "rational" part of your mind probably hooks on to a story to make it seem "real." So when your mind throws up a "what if" picture of something negative that could happen, try turning the fear in question immediately into a prayer. Don't even think about it, other than to notice it, and then turn it into a prayer for help rather than a picture of doom. For example, if you fear that it will rain, why not ask the nature spirits for sunshine? And if you want something, but you think you won't get it unless you steal it (as in the 7 of Swords), try asking the universe for what you want—directly, with humility and faith in the possibility of attaining your desire.

This may sound like simplistic advice, but whenever we scheme or plan or worry over the future, it's because we truly haven't considered that we might be able to get what we need as deserving "participants" in the balance of the whole, rather than as "control freaks" in charge of the entire operation and vying with other control freaks trying to get what they need by stealth. So try it as an experiment. Take yourself out of the active role of "driver" and put yourself in the role of "receiver" or "passenger" in a larger vehicle. If you are anxious about somebody else (it's terribly anxiety producing to try to control other people, in addition to ourselves!), then make a prayer for that person to receive what they need as well.

If your card in the future is *reversed,* this also frequently indicates the presence of doubt or fear or pessimism in regard to what's coming. Try turning the card around and meditating on it right side up. Put yourself into the picture with your imagination and try to overcome whatever doubts you feel about it through a sincere wish or a prayer. If you want your wish or prayer to be more powerful, make it in a ritual context. Bolster the mental intention to change your habitual approach by using underlying "magical" support. Go to a body of water to make your prayer—the ocean, a lake or river near your home, a special waterfall or spring that is sacred to you. Put your wishes or prayers into an object from the natural world, such as a stone, and then when you're ready, put the stone in the water and walk away *without looking back.*

Every time the fear returns to your mind and starts to make you anxious again, consciously turn it into a prayer in your mind. You can do it again and again until you are praying constantly about your problem, if need be. In this way, you begin believing in the possibility of change, rather than convincing yourself through repetition of your negative pictures that you can't have what you need. Using a "visualization" or a mantra is effective in exactly the same way, by derailing the mind from its habitual, unconscious, negative track, and then filling the vacuum with positive images and thoughts.

Esoterically, we know that what you focus your attention on is what you will manifest, whether you "want" it or not. Energy and vibration follow thought, bringing the things you think about to life. Any compulsive focus on something negative will attract more negative energy, rather than positive, into your life. This is not to say you will make your worries into reality (you would have to be quite powerful to do that), but rather that you will continue in a negative direction, making yourself more stressed and possibly "sick with worry." Worrying about the future and focusing on negative possibilities simply complicate your life unnecessarily, making you feel compressed and "tight," rather than relaxed and loose.

So go back now to the card in the future position, and see if you can put your attention on it without freaking yourself out. A Major Arcanum, of course, carries more weight and tells you about a context or situation in your future that you can't avoid. But every Major contains within the image all the information you need to know so that you can respond creatively to whatever happening or event is coming. Just as in the turning of the "year cards," there is both an energy available from the Major Arcanum as well as a teaching or task for you to learn. The task might be challenging, even difficult, but the energy to face it and learn from it comes with the task itself. When the Magician is in your future, even if you feel afraid of being spontaneous and impulsive, the energies to learn how to be that way will become available as well as the situation itself.

Esotericism tells us that we are never given anything we can't handle, and in my experience that would seem to be true. That is not to say we are not stretched to the limit at times, and even occasionally pushed past our limits, so that our old forms break and we are set free from identity, structure, and everything we have known. In the ancient cultures of the Goddess, it seems that the understanding of being part of a greater whole with an underlying order made people feel safer than we do now in our daily lives. Their anticipation of the future was perhaps not so wrought with tension as our own, or when they felt afraid, they had cultural forms and rituals for "appeasing" any displeased spirits and coming back into harmony with the whole.

Using the Motherpeace cards to look into the future can be a way of returning to this ancient consciousness that anthropologists have called "participation mystique," the understanding that we are not alone here and someone who cares about us might be listening. The cards can help us begin to repair the enormous rift we've created between ourselves and the natural world. Anytime we throw the cards (or any oracle, for that matter), we are acknowledging the invisible dimension, where all kinds of otherworldly beings exist and participate in the life of our planet. We can interact and have dialogue with them, receiving information and awakening "paranormal" senses we didn't know we had that allow us to talk to the trees, listen to the speech of birds, hear rocks singing, and see little people living under the leaves of our favorite berry patch. We can get information from this invisible dimension anytime we choose, and any such encounter is more likely than not to make us feel more included in the universe and safer in our bodies.

It is the awakening of this magical dimension of reality that caused me to name my second book about the Motherpeace a "playbook,"[13] because using the cards can bring us back into a more childlike consciousness for some very nurturing moments in our otherwise rather serious adult lives. Using the cards we can practice the simple power of prayer in our daily lives, as well as becoming familiar and grounded in the use of our intuition and instinctual (nonrational) minds. All of this leads to more balance, a stronger sense of protection and safety, and a more secure sense of being part of the whole of nature instead of some alien consciousness separate from the other life on the planet.

CHAPTER FIVE

INVOKING
GOOD
HEALTH

MEDICAL DOCTRINE ASIDE, OUR HEALTH

is directly related to our mental, emotional, and spiritual state of mind. Whether you catch the latest bug or succumb to a flu virus depends more on the condition of your immune system than on whether or not you get a flu shot, and having a healthy immune system appears to take its cues in good part from having an optimistic approach to life. It pays to keep an open heart and a well-balanced mind, so it follows that oracular practices must be helpful in achieving good health and maintaining it in daily life. You might begin to think of your Motherpeace deck as preventive medicine, and perhaps you can even turn to them when you need diagnostic advice or a cure.

In ancient times, temples that functioned as oracle centers were often places of healing as well. When a person came to incubate a dream, it might be because she was distressed and having a mental or emotional crisis, or because she was physically ill and seeking a cure. In many temples were found isolated clay body parts representing hands, feet, legs, ears, or some other part of the body that was ill and required healing. These were specific talismanic offerings to the deity of the temple, to whom a particular healing request was being made. On a trip to Malta a few years ago, our group visited a famous Church of the Virgin Mary on the smaller island of Gozo, which is still actively used today as a healing temple. In an anteroom of the sanctuary were old plaster casts, crutches, eyeglasses, and so on, all offerings left by grateful recipients testifying to the healing power of the Virgin. Petitioners can leave a donation and write their complaints or desires on slips of paper provided by the nuns, who then agree to pray daily for the healing of the ailment or the fulfillment of the desire.

Without a doubt, women were the original healers, and female-centered societies in ancient times practiced all kinds of healing rituals and ceremonies, as is evidenced in archaeological artifacts from such places as Anatolia (Turkey), Mesopotamia and Sumer (Iraq and Iran), and Old Europe. Even in Paleolithic cave sanctuaries from twenty thousand years ago, we have evidence of women dancing and performing rituals that we have every reason to believe were similar to rituals practiced by tribal people today for healing, regeneration, and renewal.

The last official temples to a healing Goddess from ancient times were classical Greek temples to Hygieia, whose name was the root of our modern word *hygiene*. The large snake climbing up her staff later became the caduceus, which is still used to represent the American Medical Association today. Hygieia was eventually replaced by male healers such as Apollo's son, Asclepius, whose dream incubation temple at Epidarus was famous all over the classical world. Women remained the midwives and primary healers for other women, however, down into the Middle Ages, when they were literally "burned out" by the Inquisition and replaced by male obstetricians using forceps for deliveries. An entire earth-based tradition of herbal medicine was wiped out at the same time and replaced by what has come to be the modern pharmaceutical industry.

Why would ancient women's religious practices be associated with curing disease? The thing most clearly missing from modern medicine's approach to illness is an acknowledgment of energy—what in acupuncture the Chinese call *chi,* and in aikido the Japanese call *ki,* and what we might call vitality or life force. This energy moves through the body in tracks or "channels" according to yogic systems of thought, similar to what an acupuncturist would describe as the "meridians" running through the physical body, which can be stimulated with special needles. In India, this specifically female energy or fire is called Shakti, meaning literally "to be able." Shakti, the name of the Goddess, is derived from a root word *(sha)* meaning "to make heat," which is also connected to *shaman.* When a female healer puts her hands on a person who is ill, the healer and patient get hot. For twenty years, I have channeled this heat that heals.

Asian systems of traditional medicine and martial arts are thousands of years old and have been practiced continuously since preliterate times, when women were the shamans. Joseph Needham's excellent text, *Science and Civilization in China,* vol. 2, documents these practices in China, and Carmen Blacker's *The Katalpa Bow* documents them in Japan. When my Chinese acupuncturist puts the needles in and turns them, she smiles and waits until I respond to what she calls a "good shock." Without such a response, she knows the needles haven't done their job of stimulating an electrical impulse at a precise anatomical point in the body that refers to a specific organ or glandular, lymph, and blood systems where the source of the problem can be found and released.

Women in the contemporary Women's Spirituality movement have been making a profound effort to rediscover and reclaim the ancient rituals and healing practices lost to us with the demise of those traditions of Goddess worship found in various parts of the world at different times. Sometimes the traditions that were part of ancient female-centered civilizations from the Neolithic period can still be perceived in the practices and world-view of contemporary tribal people, such as the Huichol Indians in Mexico, known as the "peyote people," who lived in the remote Sierra Madre mountains. Recently they were forced out of the mountains and down to the west coast of Mexico to eke out a living on pesticide-soaked tobacco plantations. The reason for their forced migrations has to do with the concept of private property and how in this century the lands were fenced in over which they have always made their annual journey to "the place where Our Mothers dwell," in order to gather the sacred peyote, which they have used in ceremonies for longer than any of them can remember. Their name means "the healers."

The Huichols are not female-centered in the sense that women govern the tribe, but symbolically they are "feminine" in their values and behaviors. Women hold a sacred place in the community, and the tribe actively worships female deities along with male ones, for example Our Mother Young Eagle Girl, who ensouls all who are born, and Grandmother Growth, to whom aspiring shamans make their offerings. All of the Huichol people are either shamans or artists—they make ceremony almost all the time! Corn is the symbolic and actual center of their tribal activity, and their agriculture is imbued with a sacred understanding, each step ritualized rather than mechanized, as in the modern way.

In a symposium on the Huichols at the Museum of Man (!) in San Diego in 1985, I gave a talk called "The Matriarchal Roots of Huichol Shamanism."[14] I consider the Huichols to be a living remnant of ancient Goddess-worshipping civilizations, probably related to the "ancient ones" who lived at Teotihuacán outside of Mexico City, which was abandoned around 600 C.E. With the influx into Mexico of the warlike Toltecs (900 C.E.) and Aztecs (1400 C.E.), the

Huichols withdrew far up into the remote mountains, where even the conquering Spanish didn't bother them. Their extreme isolation allowed them to remain in a more-or-less pristine state until very recently. Nowadays, however, beer trucks and airplanes arrive in their mountaintop homes daily. Recently one of their shamans shared a dream in which he saw that the "candles of the four corners were burning down," and it wasn't clear if the shamans would be able to continue their work of keeping those candles lit.

The Huichols, until their recent contact with Western diseases, relied on herbal medicine and shamanistic interventions (such as a small mirror or feathers) to cure all their ailments. Their sacred artistic and ceremonial callings take them on a spiritual journey not unlike those of yogis and yoginis (holy men and women) from India. The Huichols follow a protocol of serious practices and ritual vows for many years, until a certain authority and expertise is grounded in the body, at which time they become professional artists or ceremonialists on behalf of the tribal community. During their apprenticeship, they make "votive" objects and go on pilgrimages to the places where the deities are believed to live, in order to present them with offerings and take another step on the path. This is similar to what archaeology has shown us about people in the ancient cultures of Central and South America or the areas around the Mediterranean Sea from Old Europe, the Middle East, and North Africa, where the Goddess was so strong.

When you use the Motherpeace cards in readings directed at your health, you are tapping into these ancient and tribal traditions of healing, since the cards are undergirded by shamanism and women's religion. A good many of the images are based on energy-medicine and their symbolism expresses techniques or principles of natural healing practices. For more information about this, you may want to go back to *Motherpeace: A Way to the Goddess,* in which I went into greater detail about the particular meanings of each card in the deck.

In general, the usual principles apply here as in other areas: the four suits (Discs, Cups, Wands, Swords) represent the four elements (earth, water, fire, air), thereby providing information about "planes of existence" (physical, emotional, energetic, mental).

The People cards (also related to the four elements) show you yourself, your clients, your healers, and other real people in your life who are involved with your condition.

The Major Arcana give you bigger pictures of planetary or cosmic energies affecting your health, and they help you to see the larger purpose of illness or disease as well as the direction and prognosis for healing.

MOTHERPEACE FOUR-CARD READING FOR HEALTH

I have developed a simple layout for doing readings about your health on a daily basis. Using only four cards to view several different levels of reality, the reading can be as simple or profound as you want to make it. It offers a way to look at your situation with your "extra sense" and make some alterations if needed, bringing yourself into balance. I will give you the simple straightforward meanings of the four positions of the cards and, for those interested in deeper study, the esoteric side of the healing process.

You shuffle the cards as always, mixing them up and putting them facedown in preparation for choosing cards at random. As usual, you will want to create a ritual setting for yourself with an altar, candle, incense, special cloth, and so on. You want to be centered and calm, so it's good to do some sort of simple meditation or grounding process before you begin. You might want to chant one of the Goddess chants from Women's Spirituality circles. Or a Tibetan Buddhist chant to the Goddess Tara can be very helpful: OM TARA TUTTARE, TURE SO HA. This tried-and-true chant invokes the Green Tara (who protects and grants attainments), asks for her blessing, and grounds it in your heart.[15]

When you are ready, you choose four cards from anywhere in the deck and lay them out in a vertical line, one on top of another, aligned with four levels of existence: physical, emotional, mental, and spiritual (see the illustration next page).

The bottom card represents the earth plane, the physical body, and daily life. The next one directly on top of the first one represents your feelings, desires, and dreams and gives you information about the state of your emotional health. The third card is for mental health and shows you problems or well-being in the area of your attitudes, beliefs, and mental processes—that is, how you're thinking about things. The fourth card on top is for the spirit plane, and it tells you about your spiritual well-being or points to any spiritual crises that might be affecting your general health.

In a very simple way, these four cards simply give you a glimpse of yourself through the different spheres of being—your body, a mental and emotional picture, and something about your spirit. You can look at them quickly just to ascertain if there are any problems and exactly where they are located. Then you can focus on one of these four areas whatever efforts you make toward healing. For example, if all the cards seem okay except for one, then wherever that one card falls, you can think about how to modify that area of your life.

PHYSICAL PROBLEMS

If the "off" card is in the physical, and all the others seem okay, then perhaps you need something strictly physical to bring yourself back into harmony. In that case, you might get a massage or some exercise just to change your energy, or you may need to modify your diet. If the problem seems more serious or chronic, you may need to take up a new physical practice like hatha yoga, which is a gentle meditative way of stretching and affecting all the systems of the physical body. A catalytic martial arts practice such as aikido or

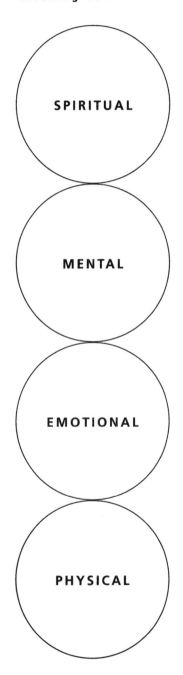

FOUR-CARD READING FOR HEALTH LAYOUT

karate might be called for if your energy is low and you feel inertia in your physical life. If discipline is all you need, it might be enough for you to take up jogging or aerobics.

EMOTIONAL PROBLEMS

If the problem occurs on the emotional level, then you might need a counseling session with a friend or a therapist. A walk in nature might cheer you up by changing your mood, or you may need to "process" something with another person about whom you are emotionally upset. Bach Flower Essences have very uplifting effects on the emotions; have a session with someone who knows the flowers and might be able to help pinpoint the area of difficulty and select the appropriate essence for you. There are also books that help you to self-diagnose with these homeopathic essences, which have no side effects and cannot hurt you. In the same vein, you might effectively transform your emotional condition by simply getting a fresh bouquet of flowers for your kitchen table or to put near your desk.

MENTAL PROBLEMS

If a problem exists on the mental level, then you need to "change your mind" in some way. If it's a temporary problem, something as simple as going to a movie can shift your outlook; so can reading a book, or having a conversation with a friend (but not necessarily about your problem). Writing in a journal can do wonders for clearing mental problems; sometimes just the uncensored process of putting your thoughts and anxieties down on paper will turn itself into a "therapy process" in which you express feelings and thoughts, observe yourself, get insights, and end up healing yourself all in one session! For more intractable mental problems, you will want to get help with unlocking the issues that are driving you crazy. If depression or anxiety are chronic, St. John's Wort extract has been shown in recent scientific studies to cure at the same rate (or better) than some of the antidepressants that would be prescribed by a conventional medical doctor, and without the side effects.

SPIRITUAL PROBLEMS

Troubles on the spiritual plane are more difficult, but once you know that this is where the problem is located, you can begin to take it seriously enough to attend to your needs through meditation, centering, and other forms of spiritual nourishment. The card may indicate a momentary bump on your spiritual path, or it could be pointing to a more serious need for spiritual intervention. It will be up to you to interpret the card, and it will vary a great deal, based on whether you are lacking a spiritual tradition or you've been practicing one for twenty years. If you don't meditate, you probably need to. Perhaps this will be the stimulus for you to go on a meditation retreat of some kind and learn a simple practice that will serve you in your daily life. If the problem is more acute, you may be suffering an actual spiritual emergency, in which case you may need help, or you will end up having to take a "dark night of the soul" journey.

So far I've just been talking about obvious problems that appear in only one place in the reading. But the reading layout allows for much more complexity, since not only are the positions meaningful (physical, emotional, mental, and spiritual), but the cards that fall there also hold a wide variety of elemental and cosmic meanings that must be integrated into the four positions. When a "mental card" falls in the emotional center, you have to take into account both mental and emotional qualities to determine the meaning. Most of us have reasonable access to the mental level where our thoughts are taking place, whereas the emotional level can be elusive and unconscious, which makes it difficult to read with the rational mind. An intellectual card in the emotional center could indicate that we are overriding our feelings with thoughts, or having feelings that are based on something we are thinking about. When an "emotional card" falls in the physical space, it shows the effect of the feelings on the physical body or tells us that the feelings are being felt or acted out through the body. And so forth. In any reading layout you are always dealing with the meanings of the cards and the overlay of meanings that you get from the positions where the cards fall in the layout.

SAMPLE READINGS

Let's say you wake up one day feeling kind of blah—no energy— with the beginnings of a sore throat, and when you do your daily health reading, these four cards show up: Priestess of Discs reversed in the first position (physical); 5 Swords in the second place (emotional); 8 of Cups upright in the third place (mental); and the Empress in the top position (spiritual).

We would suspect right away with the 8 Cups in the mental center that you are mentally depressed about something that has recently changed in a relationship. So the first thing to get in touch with is anything your partner might have done or said to make you feel bad, and any way you may have had a change of heart yourself in regard to another person. The depression could be more chronic and not related to an immediate event but to something more pervasive, like your hidden beliefs that you won't be able to get the love you need. The Priestess of Discs reversed in the physical position shows your sore throat is turning into or warning of a developing minor ailment, and you may want to treat it with extra vitamin C and garlic immediately, to prevent it from getting worse.

The 5 of Swords in the emotional position tells us you feel hurt. The nasty feeling of having been "stung" by the wasp in the card points to a hurt (unconscious, from the past, you've been hurt before) that makes you afraid you won't be able to get what you need.

SAMPLE DAILY HEALTH READING

Sometimes this card signals a defeatist attitude that may not have anything to do with anyone else; in other words, you could be paranoid. And because the emotional center is often unconscious, you might not even know you are carrying this expectation. So if you can change or shift your attitude about your situation from doubt to trust, it will be very beneficial to your overall health. We can see that partly because in the spiritual center, the Empress is right side up. Her presence in that position shows that basically everything is going well, you are well grounded and nurtured spiritually, and capable of relationship. Perhaps the healing physical energies represented by the Empress are just coming in from the spiritual level. It might take a little time for them to filter down to the physical plane (that's why the vitamin C and garlic will be certain to help).

HELPER CARDS

Since the conscious and unconscious mental attitudes seem to me the main problem here, I would suggest that after assimilating the information provided by these four cards, you also select a "helper" card from the deck, to go alongside your 5 Swords and give you a suggestion about some other way of approaching the situation. Helpers are extra cards you choose once you have worked with a card that has a "negative" message. In order to move on in your process and not get stuck in the negative message, a helper can show you the line of least resistance for changing your energy.

So let's say you choose the Son of Discs as your helper with the 5 of Swords in the emotional position. Then the suggestion is it would be good to let go of the anxiety around your problem and focus instead on a physical task of some kind, such as paying your bills, doing a focused sports activity, or working on an ongoing project you enjoy.

Or how about if the helper you select is the 3 of Cups? Then the solution will be for you to kick back, get together with friends,

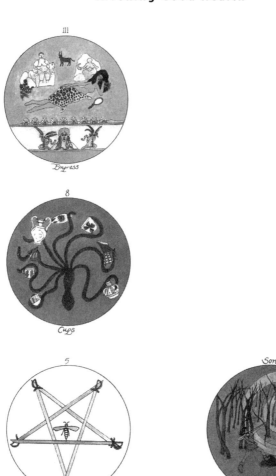

HEALTH READING WITH HELPER CARD

and go dancing or listen to music, or something else simple and fun, without any agenda, in the company of other people you enjoy. Or maybe you chose the 3 of Wands as your helper, which shows that you need to talk to someone directly and express your spontaneous truth without holding back, and this will be an antidote for your sense that you "can't" get your needs met.

You can select an unlimited number of helpers for your reading, to illuminate or expand on what the first four cards have shown you. No matter what amount of time and energy you want to spend with your reading, the helpers will provide amplification and information that will help you address your health problems. All health problems involve the emotional and mental states, which enormously affect the immune and glandular sytems. Untying the knots in your psyche can often move the energy enough to push the illness through very fast, so that in this case, your sore throat might be gone by the next day. This is especially true if the solution pertains to expressing something, either to yourself or to another person, thereby clearing the "blockage" in the throat, and moving the "dis-ease" out.

PARTICULAR AILMENTS AND DIAGNOSES

Certain cards in the deck may point to particular ailments, which might lead you to try certain natural or alternative medicines and treatments for yourself in response to the cards. For instance, if you did already have a sore throat, as in the last example, you might get information about it from such cards as Shaman of Swords reversed, 3 Wands reversed, or 7 Wands, all of which point to the need to express yourself more clearly, take a risk and tell the truth, be brave and speak from your conviction. But what if you have a sore throat and you get helper cards like 9 Discs reversed, Priestess of Swords, or Son of Cups? Then I would say you need more solitude, time for introspection and meditation, time alone to process your feelings and calm yourself, perhaps to be creative with writing. Then there are always the obvious and literal images, such as 6 Discs, which suggests bodywork or massage.

Some of the Wands (such as the 5 of Wands, the 7 of Wands, and the 10 of Wands) suggest heat or excessive energy, which might point to the causes behind an acid stomach or a headache, cramping, insomnia, or nervous agitation. Helpers to these cards (such as Cups or Discs) might indicate ways of calming the nerves, cooling the circulatory system, and quieting the mind. Swords often indicate struggle or built-up mental tension and could explain a migraine, arthritis pain, or tight muscles; helpers such as Wands (moving energy) or Discs (physical activity) could provide an antidote.

ESOTERIC UNDERPINNINGS OF HEALTH READINGS

On another level of this reading are all the principles of esoteric healing. It might help to know how to think about the movement of healing and energy from one plane to another. Generally, the planes are like "altitudes" where energies move at different frequencies, and therefore change more or less quickly, depending on the placement. We usually think of the direction of movement as taking place from the higher frequencies to the lower ones. A physical illness doesn't begin from nothing; it is often the outcome of causes that exist on other levels than the physical, which eventually impinge on that level. That's why allopathic medicine, which fails to probe the emotional and mental levels of a person's life, sometimes misses the point. On the other hand, with so many contaminants in our environment these days causing direct changes in cellular metabolism, the physical plane can affect other planes as well. In this way, the force of illness moves in the opposite direction.

PHYSICAL PLANE

The first card in the physical position indicates energies moving on the physical plane, which move in slow waves that appear more dense to us, even solid. It takes longer for something to manifest physically, but it also takes longer to get rid of it once it has taken shape on that level. A sore throat could be the beginning of a serious manifestation of something that has probably been "wrong" for a while on other planes (like the instances of not expressing the truth or speaking out, which I dealt with earlier). Tumors and cellular changes are the extreme example of this kind of long-term manifestation process that eventually produces some sort of substance on the physical plane (in the physical body).

EMOTIONAL PLANE

Illness taking shape on the emotional level might be felt at first as depression, inertia, exhaustion, even hopelessness, and later as glandular or organ problems (thyroid deficiency, adrenal exhaustion, weakness, pain or infection of the kidneys). Hormonal upsets for women are closely bound to emotions and fall into this category, which includes painful menstruation, PMS, or heavy bleeding, hot flashes, itching, breast lumpiness or pain. The liver is tied in with the hormones in a fairly direct way, so if emotional problems go on for a while, they can end up manifesting as liver ailments directly related to the liver (jaundice, swelling, and pain) or secondary ailments, such as fibroids in the uterus or breast, skin eruptions or rashes, or eye infections.

An added complexity here is that the liver is trying to process environmental toxins as well because the female hormonal-emotional system has to contend with pollution and the rampant use of pesticides, plastics, radiation, and other contaminants in our environment. Theo Colburn's brilliant book *Our Stolen Future* shows that many chemicals mimic estrogen and bond to our cells in damaging ways that affect the liver function, as well as creating cell mutations. I sometimes wonder if women aren't depressed because our bodies are having to process the damage done to the environment in such a direct way, both emotionally and physically, simply because it is not possible for our intricate hormonal systems to separate the two. Women suffer from so-called environmental and autoimmune illnesses in much higher numbers than men.

MENTAL PLANE

Energies from the mental plane affect our nervous systems, our brains, and our spinal cords. Discord on the mental level that continues becomes long-term stress and creates illness, especially those such as arthritis and joint problems, stiff necks, headaches, migraines, and eye problems. Even heart disease is affected by mental stress, as has been shown in biofeedback experiments. The mental plane pertains to pictures we hold in our minds, old beliefs that condition us to act in certain ways that may not be in our best long-term interest, and mental programming that we don't even know we have.

One of the most serious problems with our present medical establishment was pointed out by Jean Achterberg in her book, *Imagery in Healing: Shamanism and Modern Medicine.* She describes the power that doctors' disease pictures can have on patients, and how a diagnosis and prognosis can actually make a patient worse if the patient takes the negative picture into herself and "complies" with the expectation it holds. The idea of degenerative illnesses such as MS, lupus, Parkinson's, and so on seems very negative in this light, providing a perfectly clear image for a patient to focus on in a totally negative way. Doctors tell patients exactly what symptoms they can expect a little way down the road, and as Achterberg points out, patients tend to comply because their minds become engaged in a process of (negative) creative visualization.

Esoteric wisdom would describe the pictures as filtering down through the planes from the mental to the emotional level (depression, fear, anxiety, hopelessness—all of which have negative effects on the immune system), and ultimately to the physical plane (the body itself), which then manifests the symptoms suggested by the hypnotist-doctor. You can see then how important it is to clear negative mental issues (the third position in the reading layout) in order to further physical well-being.

SPIRITUAL LEVELS

When spirit calls us, we must respond, or else we become ill eventually. This is the worldwide understanding of people called to a shamanic vocation, as demonstrated in Joan Halifax's wonderful early book, *Shamanic Voices*. The spiritual plane is the "highest" one in our reading layout and therefore the most distant one from any manifestation of physical illness, but because the frequency of the vibration on the spiritual level is so fast, it can effect change on the physical plane almost immediately. This is the nature of "spontaneous healing" when illness miraculously disappears through some unknown means, as Andrew Weil has shown in his book by that name.

In alternative medicine, practitioners are aware of this level of reality and are always helping clients to search for the deepest level of meaning behind any illness. Healers who channel energies for healing the body, mind, or emotions are bringing strong vibrations from the spiritual level to the lower levels where it can transform the patterns there. If you get a negative card in the spiritual position, or your card is upside down, it suggests that you could affect the problem by using the power of prayer or spiritual channeling. It might show a spiritual crisis happening in your life, or a profound change of direction, such as in a shamanic healing crisis. A physical card there (Discs) could suggest you need a radical change of diet and accompanying lifestyle; an emotional card (Cups) could suggest you need expressive bodywork, acupuncture, or Bach flowers; a mental card (Swords) might mean you need to meditate to still the discursive mind so you can hear a message from a higher level. Remember, you can always choose a Helper card for any images that seem to indicate dis-ease.

Often the card in the spiritual center is the one that helps us to learn to trust the Goddess and stop our ceaseless worrying. Any positive image in that position shows us that you are being aided from invisible levels, and that soon you will feel better by just letting that spiritual force into your reality. Another way of thinking about it is that your "high self" is handling the problem and your job is simply to turn it over. This is the essential purpose of any oracle in the final analysis, to help you relax and accept your fate or else effect a change, whatever is "in the cards."

CHAPTER SIX

RELATIONSHIPS
AND THE
MOTHERPEACE
CARDS

RELATIONSHIPS SEEM TO BE EVERY-
body's "big issue" in our time. Clients who come to me for readings are naturally interested in their careers, projects, spiritual
paths, children, and so on, but practically every woman I see is pri-
marily concerned over the challenge of finding the right relationship and maintaining it successfully. Most of us seem to feel that
whatever inabilities we have in this area are personal and can be
solved by trying harder, doing better, or going further in some way.
I tend to feel that the whole issue of relationship (or "relatedness")
has broken down for everyone partly as a result of our culture's
tremendous focus on individuality, personal control, and self-
reliance. Our fundamental shift away from nature during the classical period in Greece, and the accompanying dualism of spirit over
matter, mind over body, and male over female has left us alone with
our existential anxiety.

In the Motherpeace cards, Karen Vogel and I attempted to imagine relationships and interactions not bound by twentieth-century rules and expectations of behavior. Our ideas were informed by images from Paleolithic caves, information about burials from Neolithic sites, and written and artistically rendered narratives from the later Bronze and Iron Ages around the Mediterranean, as well as anthropological reports about tribal people still alive in the last two or three centuries in the Americas, Africa, Australia, Russia, Europe, and Asia. From this wide range of material, we observed certain consistent themes.

Relationships have changed immensely since the ancient cultures that worshipped the Goddess and lived in peaceful, egalitarian centers of agriculture and animal husbandry. Archaeological evidence shows that in many places in ancient times men and women often didn't live together in the same buildings, so that whatever heterosexual pair-bonding went on, it happened in an entirely different context from today's nuclear family structure. It's hard to imagine, from our modern point of view, what it must have been like to spend the majority of our days in the company of other women, sharing work and child rearing in a communal spirit of pulling together. Certainly men came and went in an organic, inclusive way in these ancient societies, but it was women who were at the center and held the roles of priestess and, as a natural extension of their mothering, positions on the governing council.

In thinking about the prototypical relationships that would have developed in such a context, it is important to grasp that these female-centered societies—with the exception of much later Amazon cultures—were not "matriarchal" in some reverse sense of patriarchy, where women dominated or held power over men. Early cultures like those at Catalhöyük and Jericho (seventh millennium B.C.E.) were communal, egalitarian, nonhierarchical, and peaceful—the struggle for domination had not yet begun. Certain questions that emerge from this evidence have fascinated me for most of my adult life. Within the ancient "matristic" context, for example, what would a personal relationship look like? How, I wonder, did they experience "romantic" love (if at all), and how did they reconcile potential differences (if they felt them)? Were they monogamous, in any sense of the word as we use it?

All of this is background material for those of us using the Motherpeace cards today to examine our relationships and receive oracles pertaining to them. Women in the West have certain freedoms we take for granted, such as the right to choose a partner based on our own feelings, desires, and the agendas we have set for our lives. Yet we are also bound by the model of hierarchical romantic love that was artificially developed at the beginning of classical Greek civilization based on the idea of a passive love object. In the Athenian model of marriage, men were privileged over women in blatant ways that were written into laws and religious codes of the times, and that have come down to us as our modern legacy. It's fairly well documented by now that Athenian women were locked in their homes without a vote or participation as citizens at all, while the men gathered in public places, held symposia, made love with one another, and kept courtesans, called hetqerae, for their heterosexual pleasure.

In the Motherpeace Lovers (VI) card (see illustration next page), Karen Vogel worked with the development of romantic love as invented by the Greeks in the fifth century B.C.E. The two Greek vases portray the dualistic way that women were perceived, as submissive objects of affection or enemies needing to be dominated.

As the disciplines of history and archaeology have evolved in the last two decades, we know now that the Greeks came into contact with many other cultures that did not treat women as chattel (property), and that anytime they encountered such groups of people, they referred to them as "barbarians," in the main because of the freedom women had in those foreign cultures. Greek historians describe women in other cultures as having equal rights to hold property and do business, ride horses, lead troops into battle, rule kingdoms, and generally carry on as bona fide citizens. They were consistently shocked and outraged by this confrontation, as the tremendous number of images of Greeks fighting Amazons demonstrates.

For the Greeks, there were two models of romantic love, which are portrayed in the two vases in the Lovers card. On the right, we see a man dancing away with a woman, either sweeping her off her feet, or in less pleasant but more frequent depictions, abducting her to be his "wife." Such abductions (sometimes described more literally as rapes) were common to the Greeks, who were bolstered by the mythologies of that prolific rapist, Zeus, and the famous and much-glorified rape of Persephone by Pluto, the underworld deity. In the vase on the left, we see the hero slaying the Amazon Queen, an image that can refer to either Theseus and Penthesilea from the Trojan War (1200 B.C.E.), or to Achilles and Hippolyta (or Antiope) from slightly later. We are told in all the commentaries describing the vase paintings that the hero "fell in love" with the mighty Amazon queen at the moment that he murdered her. Two thousand years later we have the movie *Looking for Mr. Goodbar* as an indication of that unbroken tradition, which still binds us.

So this is our legacy and the mythological roots of our modern practices of "falling in love." Either we wait for that moment when we can blissfully surrender ourselves into the hands of another who presumably will take care of us, or we fight to the death for control over ourselves as autonomous beings (Amazons) in exile from the power of love. Many modern women have tried both scripts without much luck in the deep searching that has taken place since the sexual revolution of the 1960s, when we were supposedly liberated from the narrow moral-sexual codes of earlier generations. Our monogamous commitments "till death do us part" have become the ritual litanies of multiple relationships lived out as a serial monogamy repeated every few years.

And so we come to the oracles for help. Where is my true love, my soul mate, my compatible life partner? How can I find him or her? How can I do the work of making myself ready and capable of such a relationship, and what are the qualifications needed for the task? Can I influence another person to love me more? To choose me over someone else? Can I influence the Fates to bring my love to me sooner, rather than later, and will the Fates intervene if my relationship is in danger of collapsing? Is it even possible for two self-centered individuals to come together in harmony and form a complementary relationship in the late twentieth century?

MOTHERPEACE RELATIONSHIP READING

Because of the intense importance women place on these questions of relationship, I have developed a variety of ways to read the cards for couples or individuals who are looking into relationship questions. In the *Motherpece Tarot Playbook* I shared a very complicated chakra reading to be done between two people. The layout I will share in this chapter is simple, straightforward, and fun to experience (together or separately). At the same time, it allows for the possibility of seeing quite deeply into the relationship patterns, the psyches of the two individuals, their dynamic interplay, and the often hidden purpose of the relationship itself.

INDIVIDUALS

This short reading allows you to check into any of your relationships at any time, to see what the dynamics are between any two people—you and a partner, you and someone you just met, or you and one of your children, parents, friends, or business partners. If you are interested in practicing with the cards, you can ask about any or all of your relationships every morning before you encounter these people during the day. Then at the end of the day, you can come back to the readings and see how the predictions the cards made turned out "in real life." This is a great way for women to deal with what can often seem like an obsessional focus on relationships because you'll be learning a new language (the Motherpeace cards) instead of just feeding your addiction!

THE READING

Set up your ritual environment in whatever way you like, with sage or incense, a candle, a nice clean surface on which to lay out the cards, and so on. Then shuffle the cards as always and lay them out in a circle facedown. As a meditation, see if you can "call in" a clear image of the other person involved in the relationship and hold that image in your mind as you lay out the cards. The layout is as follows: three cards for *each* person, laid out vertically, one row next to the other, as if the cards were representing you on the left and the other person on the right side.

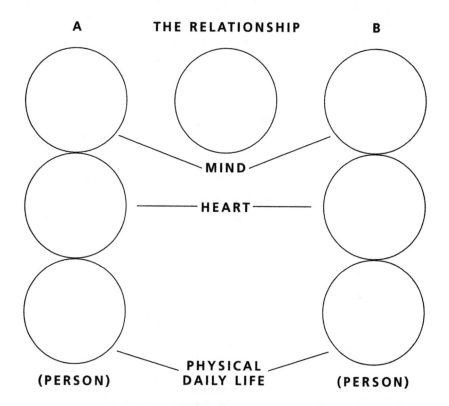

RELATIONSHIP READING LAYOUT

The bottom card in each row represents you and the other person, specifically in relation to each other, on the physical plane or in daily life. The middle cards show you and the other person, in relation to each other, on the heart level. And the top two cards show you and the other person, in relation to each other, on the level of consciousness or the mind. Finally, you select one card at random to represent the relationship itself—separate from either of you— and you place it at the top, where it links the two people together at the spirit level.

Take your time with the reading, since seven cards is a fairly large number of images and positions to handle. Begin with the bottom level, and go up from there. This level represents the daily life and what is visible, including behavior, actions, things you say to each other, and so forth. This is also the level that other people are seeing, or the public aspect of your relationship. Sometimes the cards at this level will show the immediate problems that have caused you to ask the question, such as a fight you've just had or some way that one or the other is behaving that is catalyzing a crisis.

Notice whether the cards here are Major Arcana or Minor, so that you have a sense of whether the two of you are under any planetary or cosmic influences in the sphere of your daily life interactions. Having any of the Majors here will indicate that the behaviors are much more important than otherwise. If you both have Majors, then you are pretty much in the hands of the Fates rather than being able to act with autonomy. And if one of you has a Major Arcanum and the other does not, this may help you to have some sympathy for whichever partner is experiencing the "bigger" energies, which often stimulate us to act in ways we feel we cannot control. If both cards are Minor Arcana, then things are fairly flexible and open to change or intervention.

Go on to the second level, the level of the heart, where often you can see the deeper intention on the part of each person, and the loving connection that exists behind the problems being acted out on the physical plane. Major Arcana here indicate soul contact and sometimes show that the souls of the two people are being affected by fateful energies and forces that drive them to change or transform in some way with regard to the other person or the relationship itself. Reversed cards or smaller cards from the Minor Arcana show us whether or not our hearts are open to the other person, and vice versa.

Sometimes one person will appear open on one level and not the other, and the other person will be open or closed in the opposite place, making for significant gaps in the communication between the partners. Seeing this kind of temporary incompatibility may not give you the power to intervene or change the basic facts (or, for that matter, the other person), but it might give you compassion and the understanding needed to be patient with your partner or yourself. It helps tremendously in relationship work to begin to see that the other person, whom we love to blame for all the problems in the relationship, isn't any more "wrong" than you yourself. If neither of you is wrong, and each of you is open to the other person (although not necessarily on the same level or in the same way), then there is hope for improvement without thinking you have to change yourself or the other person.

Now go to the third level—the consciousness or mental plane—and look at the cards here. Using the same criteria as with the earlier cards, see if the two people are open to each other, are ruled by "fate" cards or are working with more personal energies. Are you and your significant other holding positive or negative pictures of each other, seeing each other in a basically good light or otherwise? Is either of you silently angry with the other? Depressed, hurt, or thinking hopeless thoughts about the relationship? Withdrawn or turning away? Happy and detached, going about his or her business, thinking everything is perfectly okay?

Sometimes the pictures in the cards—especially the People cards—will show very literal body language that you can read as scenarios between the two of you. For instance, if the Son of Discs is on the right side of the reading (representing an "other" in relation to you), his body language indicates that he is focused in a direction facing away from you, either on the tasks at hand or someone else.

If the Priestess of Cups is there, she's facing you and experiencing a great longing in your direction. Daughter of Wands is running toward you, but Priestess of Swords is walking away.

On your side, the Daughter of Discs is in her own space, seeking help, whereas the Daughter of Swords is doing everything in her power to get the attention of the partner.

The numbered cards can also be read in this literal, visual way. Let's say you have the 8 of Swords in your reading on one side or the other, which shows there is a blockage or obstacle that one of you is experiencing in the relationship. But if the card shows up reversed, then it shows a breakthrough or tells you that something has just opened up for that person. See the illustrations next page. But even without knowing the traditional meaning of the card, you still can get lots of information from just the visual image of the fence or wall in the picture, which first closes things in and then opens things up.

UPRIGHT

REVERSED

The 5 of Swords is similar: when upright it shows a pentagram facing downward, the traditional hexing position, and when reversed, the pentagram is an upright five-pointed star of blessing.

When you've achieved some understanding of the dynamics between you and the other person, turn to the single card at the top that represents the relationship. If this were an entity on its own, separate from either of you, what would be its experience? A Major Arcanum will carry a lot of weight, showing that the relationship is under the power of the Fates. A less powerful card will show a more temporary situation, allowing you to see "which way the wind is blowing" in the relationship itself. Quite often, in spite of whatever problems and irritations show up in the individual readings, the relationship itself will look great. If this is the case, there is really nothing to worry about, the problems will probably pass of their own accord, the way so many things do with time.

SOLVING RELATIONSHIP PROBLEMS

However, if problems show up in the relationship, then there may be something going on that is beyond your comprehension or control. Deep and significant relationships are karmic, having many levels of interaction available in time and space, including hidden causes and things we can't see from past lives. Sometimes trouble on this larger level of the relationship will blow over like a thunderstorm or hurricane, without you ever really knowing on a conscious level what happened. If you know that a problem exists and what it looks like, you can sometimes make a unilateral change in the dynamic by acting differently, saying something, or changing the picture you hold of the other person.

For couples (and sometimes close friends or family relationships), there may be a need for a therapeutic intervention of some sort. The two of you might go into counseling together, or address your issues together in some way (perhaps using the cards), or even take a retreat or vacation as an experimental time-out from mundane activities to see if being together in more relaxed, closer contact might solve the problems. If the situation between you is not at a disabling or catastrophic level, you may be able to agree to use a session with the Motherpeace cards as a counseling device to help you sort out some of your issues, work through disagreements or misunderstandings, and renew your healthy communication.

MOTHERPEACE COUPLE'S RITUAL
COUNSELING SESSION

If you decide to try a self-counseling session for your relationship, then there are some ground rules that will make it more likely to succeed. First of all, establish a central altar that represents the relationship itself as a kind of entity or "container" for the two of you. This can be an elaborate affair that you set up with candles, flowers, images, personal items from each of you, and so on, or it can be as simple as a single lit candle. The point is you agree to surrender your hearts to the relationship itself on the highest level of its manifestation and purpose, and you deliberately come to the altar of your relationship together as equals. This keeps both of you humble, open, and compassionate to yourselves and each other.

Allow an open-ended time for this ritual in order to help it be effective. Begin by taking time to ground and center yourselves individually, sitting together in silence and finding your place in the room or in a natural setting, in relation to each other and the altar that represents your container. If you are angry with each other, you don't have to pretend to be friendly or lovey-dovey; just come together in an agreed-upon truce based on the loving commitment the two of you made in a prior state of harmony, which is represented by the altar you've created. It is to this deeper harmony that you are wishing to return, through the magical transformation of a ritual process that can lead you there when neither of you knows how to make peace happen by yourself.

Once you have individually settled yourselves in the space and found your centers, begin the process of working through your grievances by taking turns shuffling the Motherpeace cards without talking or raising any issues. If you can, use the quiet time for praying on behalf of the relationship—that it might be renewed, refreshed, and returned to harmony through your combined actions. If you share a sense of deity or source, then you can make these prayers explicit if you like, each giving voice to your individual wishes and intentions for the relationship. If any part of your disagreement or incompatibility is around the whole definition of deity and spirituality, then it will be more effective to use very general concepts, such as the "Universe," when praying together.

When you are ready, spread the cards out in a circle facing down, and each of you select three cards to represent the three levels of reality for yourself in relation to the other person—the earthly, physical reality; the emotional, heart-and-soul reality; and the mental or consciousness level of reality. Place these images faceup in the vertical placement described earlier. One of you can select the card to represent the relationship and place it at the top, or if it seems too difficult to decide which one of you will do that (and becomes part of the problem you're trying to work out), then each of you choose a card to represent the container, and you'll have two images to work with, both of which will be expressive of the relationship.

Now sit for a little while in silence and take in the whole reading layout. Sometimes the reading will be so obvious or funny in some way that it will make you both laugh and help break the ice, but if it doesn't, don't worry. Just decide who will start, and begin to read the cards from the pictures. Remember to breathe. It helps very much for each person to read his or her own cards and make only "I" statements, rather than crossing over to the other side of the reading to make generalizations about the partner. Trust each other to be able to speak for yourselves.

Using the cards should lead to opportunities to unveil yourself, seeing yourself as you are—puffed up or exaggerated, paranoid, judgmental and critical, or just withdrawn—and these characteristics become pretty obvious. The thing about doing the reading with two people together is that you each witness the other, and the layout offers opportunities to see the ways in which each of the partners is here open, there closed, in one aspect loving and forgiving, but on another level, spiteful and shut down. Usually the overall effect of a couple's reading done in good faith is to create a context in which each person experiences being "busted" at some point, in the sense of shattering the unconscious position you hold that says you're okay and the other person is to blame. This disruption in your habitual way of thinking gives you back the capacity to appreciate the other person once more.

As in any therapeutic encounter, if there is tension and mistrust, then be very careful about staying with the "I" statements and staying away from blaming "you" statements. Listen thoroughly to the other person when it is his or her turn, without interrupting or interjecting your opinions, responses, reactions, and so on. Honor each other by holding the assumption that the other person's reality is as valid to them as your own is to you, even if it doesn't agree with your view of the situation at all. Simply try to hear each other; this is the crucial key to the success of the ritual.

Finally, work with the central card(s) representing the relationship itself. Imagine that the relationship is almost like a person with its own agendas and purpose, and that the image(s) you are seeing reflects the current state of that purpose. Take turns giving your perspective on the card(s) and see if you can reach a genuine consensus. If this is able to happen, the release of tension that accompanies it will set you both free to enjoy each other's company and relax in the healing energy that naturally flows from such a moment. Take advantage of it and be affectionate with each other, letting touch and intimacy further enhance the feeling of connectedness you have managed to attain through your ritual. Be grateful and express this gratitude to the "Universe" or whatever beings or energies you originally prayed to for guidance and help. Close the ritual by blowing out the candle or thanking the invisible helping spirits.

If you are not so fortunate as to reach this kind of trans-
formed experience through the ritual, simply remain in a state of
respectful awareness of each other and your right to disagree.
Maybe the card you drew to represent the relationship itself was
negative or catastrophic, such as the Tower or the 10 of Swords or
the Devil.

This still doesn't mean the relationship is over, or that you
haven't any choices. It simply indicates a stalemate in the present
moment and difficulties that—although perhaps not insurmount-
able—will need to be faced and dealt with seriously. Allow the
images from any disturbing cards to stay with you, to sink into
your deeper consciousness for a period of time. Be together with
this confrontation from the oracle. Don't assume you know the
outcome, but rather that—like a Zen practitioner—you Don't
Know. Let the depth of this awareness penetrate through all the
levels of your reality.

You can still close the ritual by thanking any helping energies
or forces, blow out the candle, and separate in the trust that this
good-faith effort will not be in vain. Whatever issues you have each
been able to bring to the attention of the other person, and whatever deeper level of alignment with the forces of fate that you may
have attained through the ceremony, will continue to work in your
lives after you open the circle and blow out the candle. Consciousness and communication are worth the effort. Mutual respect is the
right approach under any conditions, no matter what the final
outcome.

This crisis-intervention counseling ritual using the Motherpeace cards can be repeated as often as you like, perhaps becoming
a part of your spiritual practice as a couple. A monthly "check-in"
on a sacred level does wonders for any relationship and could
become the preliminary preparation for regular, deeper Tantric
practices that could transform and illuminate the otherwise routine
interactions any couple gets into after the honeymoon phase. The

important thing is the genuine equality between partners that you structure into the relationship through these practices, as well as, to resist stagnation, the attention given to communication and exchange on an ongoing and dynamic level.

MANIFESTING A NEW RELATIONSHIP

If you don't have a partner and wish that you did, you can use the Motherpeace cards to help you envision, invite, and create the relationship you are dreaming about. Once again, create a ritual space by lighting candles, burning smudge or incense, and having a beautiful place for laying out the cards. Center yourself and shuffle the cards for as long as you like, letting your imagination begin to actively picture your ideal mate (or date!). Think of all the qualities you appreciate in another person, the ways you wish a partner would treat you, and if you like, you can even focus on physical attributes or types that appeal to you. Let your fantasies go wild while you mix the cards, and then fan them out into a great circle around you, and sit in the middle.

When you are ready, begin to create a composite lover by choosing one card at a time and placing it in front of you. But each time you finish looking at the card you just selected, turn a little bit in one direction, so that you choose the next card from that place, and then turn some more, and choose another card, until you have turned in a complete circle and have chosen twenty-one cards. These twenty-one cards will collectively describe the person you are drawing into your life through the magic of manifestation. They will show you aspects of your unconscious that you may not be aware of, so some of the cards may not be what you expect. For example, you probably will not like all the cards you choose.

Don't panic, but do work with the images you find negative or unattractive. These are showing you "karmic seeds" that exist in your psyche and that function in a compulsive way to bring the wrong qualities into your life again and again, because you haven't released the underlying cause yet. On the way out of a failed relationship you say that you will "never do that again!" But then, before you know it, you've constellated a new relationship with a seemingly new person, yet suddenly you're both behaving as if you are in some old crummy movie that you wish you didn't have to watch again. This is the way "scripts" work in our lives, and how we find ourselves trapped in sex-role stereotypes or other negative patterns that seem preconditioned—because they are!

So use this opportunity to do some transformation work on your unconscious mind, cleaning out some of the scripts you took in as a small child from telelvision, movies, your parents, as well as the church, school, and other institutions you have been a part of. Once you have the twenty-one cards faceup, go around the circle a second time and get rid of some of them. Study the ones you hate, turn them right side up if they're reversed, open yourself to the information available in even the worst ones. Then throw away seven of them. Now, after breathing deeply, do this one more time—going again around the circle and throwing out seven more images after appreciating the information they have to offer you. See if you can become conscious of your patterns, the choices you tend to make, and the unconsious pulls to what is not in your interest.

Now, take the remaining seven cards and place them in a vertical line, so that they look vaguely like a person. You can do this one of two ways: you can mix the cards and choose the positions without looking at the images, so that the composite person you invent is a "random" expression of your unconscious inner mind. Or you can deliberately create this composite partner by placing the remaining seven cards in whatever positions (or chakras if you like) you choose. Make this person as real as you can with your imagination, and as pleasing as possible to your romantic and emotional self. Is this a person you would like to spend your life (or an evening) with? Then take some time at the end of this ritual to "make it true" by holding the visualization until you can feel your desire reeling it in. Say "so be it," and blow out the candle.

Now the only thing to avoid in this kind of "spell" is that you never do this kind of magic on a person you already know you want. If you do, it will become part of your unconscious karmic process in an even more negative way, because (1) you are forcing your will on another person, and (2) you are limiting the help that the universe can give you. Keep it open, make it general, and allow the universal forces to work at their level (instead of yours) to bring you the best possible partner or relationship. Blessed Be.

CHAPTER SEVEN

THE
MOTHERPEACE
YES-NO READING

AT THOSE TORTUOUS TIMES WHEN you are simply unable to make a decision about something, when you can't tell, no matter how many times you turn the question over in your mind, which way to go or how to make the "right" decision—is it yes, or is it no; should you do it, or should you not—I generally use a special "yes-no" layout. This layout can break through the logjam when I am tired from the struggle of trying to weigh the pros and cons of a situation, and I cannot for the life of me see clearly into the situation, and I am truly ready to allow the universe (my higher self) to make the decision for me. My rational mind just gives up. It also helps if the question is in some sense "black and white," leaning toward a clear answer one way or the other. When I feel resigned to going either way with it, I ask the cards and accept the answer as my fate.

The peace that comes at the end of ambivalence is worth the price of rational control. However, this kind of process is not to be done casually, and it is not for the faint-hearted questioner. Be certain you are ready to give up any attachment to the outcome. You have to be ready to turn it over to the wisdom of the universe when you ask the yes-no question, because you may not get the answer you are hoping for. It can be quite devastating to think you're ready for the cards to give you the advice you seek, and then to receive a definite answer that doesn't fit your picture. And if you ask the cards a yes-no question and then ignore what they tell you, it is likely to haunt you, which only adds to the tortured quality of the situation.

This is the format you turn to when disturbed or agitated, when you cannot find a centered place in yourself to quiet the noisy mind in order to find a solution on your own. So you come to the cards with a humble heart, needing help and knowing it. In this way, you participate with the ancients in putting the question to someone else (in this case the cards) to help you resolve a disturbing or anxiety-producing situation in which you feel helpless to make a rational decision for yourself. When you do this, you are practicing "divination," which is usually defined by scholars as a science apart from "oracles"—those messages or communications from the spirit world that come spontaneously and unbidden.

In very ancient times, when people were connected to nature and felt themselves to be held in the deep structure I described in earlier chapters, they viewed the signs and omens of the natural world as direct messages from the Fates. In the Motherpeace deck, the Crone is an image of someone walking through life in such a simple, open way, listening for oracles and receiving the wisdom available through the whispering of the wind, shooting stars, and other messages from the night sky, signposts along the path, and the voices you hear in the silence of your quiet mind. If you can learn the art of meditation and contemplation, you will be more available to hear the communications that are always being made from another dimension.

But divination—the purposeful act of "divining" the future, or more precisely, receiving the answer to a specific question—is a more deliberate and conscious action taken by the questioner; it is somewhat out of the ordinary and one step removed from the earlier "participation mystique." In the transition to a more rational worldview during classical times, temples had become places where people came to ask priestesses (and even later priests) to divine the answer to their questions for them. The question or request being made was important enough to warrant a pilgrimage to the temple for that purpose, with offerings made to the deity of the temple, and sometimes entailed even sleeping in the temple precinct, where you might receive a dream or visionary message from the spirit world.

Apropos of our yes-no reading, the ancients had many forms of divination in which the response could be either yes or no. This is the generalized meaning of "drawing lots," the forms for which varied across cultures and down through the millennia. At Delphi during classical times, the priestess had a dish of white and black beans. In response to an inquiry on the part of the person who had made a pilgrimage to the oracular temple to ask a question, she would without looking pick out of this dish a bean of one color or the other. Her choice of either white or black bean indicated an answer of either yes or no. The Greek word for any kind of divinatory answer means literally "to pick up," and seems to have been derived from this practice.[16]

Delphi was an active oracular site since at least the Late Bronze Age (1500 B.C.E.), when according to folklore, the oracle was transported from Crete to the mainland. Almost certainly, at this earlier oracle the priestess still performed her prophetic function in a more natural, communal way, providing information for the community and warnings about the future without the later formalized process of drawing lots or deliberately stimulating a response. It was around 1500 B.C.E. that the Cretan culture was disintegrating, the great volcano that was the island of Thera (modern Santorini) exploded, and the power shifted to the Mycenaean culture on the mainland.

The oracle at Delphi originally belonged to Gaea, the Earth Mother, as it had belonged to Rhea (mother of Zeus) in Crete. It seems almost certain that the Delphic priestess (more likely *priestesses,* since the early rituals were collective female ecstatic rites) gave their original "mantic" responses in the large Corycian cave above the classical site where temples were later built to Athena and Apollo. Similarly, rituals had been practiced in the caves on Crete for millennia, at least since the time of the Neolithic Snake Goddesses that were found on that island.

The Corycian cave—where nymphs, maenads, and wild women once held their orgiastic Dionysian rites—has been so long out of popular use that when Demetra George and I first took a group of women to visit the site in the early 1990s, it turned out that our bus driver didn't actually know where it was. Our big tour bus ended up precariously perched on the edge of the mountain while the thirty-five of us walked the rest of the way on foot to the famous cave. When we arrived at the sacred place, we gathered outside the entrance to enact the first of our modern improvisational rituals for reclaiming some of what we felt our ancient foremothers might have experienced there.

Demetra George pioneered feminist astrology, using the thousands of asteroids now available to astrologers including many with names of goddesses, nymphs, and mythological creatures, as well as place-names such as Delphi.[17] We had divided our group into five smaller groups based on each woman's personal astrology chart and which asteroids were most significant for her, and each group had collectively prepared something to share with the larger group in the ritual. The Drakonia group began the ritual by guarding the entrance to the cave, as appropriate to their namesake, Drakonia, the ancient female dragon said to be the guardian of the oracular site. This certainly refers to the "dragon currents" in the earth recognized by ancient religions everywhere and acknowledged today in Chinese geomancy.

As we made our way past them into the cave, each of the other groups in turn presented their portion of the loosely planned, highly improvisational event, with the Gaea group welcoming us back into the ancient earth-womb, the Pythia group helping us to become receptive to any prophetic messages that we might receive in the silence of the ancient place, and the Dionysian nymphs and maenads leading us in an orgiastic dance of celebration at the end. By the time we came back out of the cave and into the bright sunshine, we had truly entered an altered, ecstatic state, as witnessed by the fact that when I went to do a handspring in the circle (as I often do when our rituals are at a high point), I almost fell off the mountain as a result of the subtle inner shift in my equilibrium. Others were similarly off balance.

We are told by historians that it was in the eighth century B.C.E. that Apollo took over this oracular center by slaying the Python by whose power and authorization the Pythia (the Delphic priestess) had made her pronouncements. In the tradition of Gilgamesh of Sumeria and Marduk of Babylonia, later to be repeated by those "sainted" dragon-slayers George and Michael, the hero always has to kill the monster of "snake power," which belongs to the ancient lineage of female priestesses, in order to usurp their power and authority for himself. By classical times, the oracular process had been codified to the point where the Pythia was operating in name only and was no longer directly tapping into the powerful earth currents or "dragon lines." It was probably only then that she would simply reach in a basket and draw lots by pulling out a yes-no answer for the pilgrim.

The tradition has survived to modern times in the unfortunate practice of "blackballing," which occurs in the twentieth century in our secret societies, such as the Rainbow Girls, a group I briefly joined as a young high school girl in Mt. Vernon, Iowa. "Who can belong to Rainbow Girls?" the question was put to each initiate. "Any good girl past the age of twelve" was the required answer. A box containing many white balls and one black one was passed around the assembly hall, and any girl could—for any reason—"blackball" a girl who was aspiring to become part of the coveted inner circle of Rainbow Girls. Needless to say, we had no idea that this rather nasty practice was at least as old as the Delphic Oracle with her white beans and black ones!

So-called games of chance have been around since at least the time of the Sumerians, and the casting of lots is mentioned in the texts, including the Bible, of every ancient culture of which we have records. In the archaeological museum in Cairo, I saw such a board game in the shape of a snake from predynastic Egypt (before 3000 B.C.E.). The flights of birds and shooting stars (whether they fell or flew from right to left, or vice versa) were read as yes-no responses to questions posed. The "dunking" method or "river ordeal" is mentioned by scholars for Babylonians accused of crimes. If the person sank, he was guilty; if he floated, he was considered innocent.[18] A disturbing twist on this already questionable method was used by Catholic priests during the Inquisition in Europe for dealing with the supposed guilt or innocence of the thousands of women they accused of being witches. In a remarkable version of "damned if you do, damned if you don't," a woman who drowned was proven innocent, whereas if she floated, she was guilty of witchcraft and burned at the stake.

One of the most interesting methods of obtaining a yes-no answer to a question is the divining by arrows, which is still practiced by Tibetans. Two arrows are tied with scarves—a white and a black one—representing yes and no, good and bad, positive and negative values. On a white woolen cloth, a handful of barley is poured out, and the two arrows are "thrust point downwards into the barley." The diviner concentrates with mantras and practices forms of what would be called dowsing in the West, or telekinesis. After a time, in a process that hearkens back to my early experiences of using a Ouija board, the two arrows "begin to move without any apparent physical force being applied to them," and the pattern of their movements is interpreted by the diviner.[19]

Similarly in Islamic Iraq, in the Ka'bah of Mecca, there was a game of Seven Arrows in which one of the arrows had written on it *yes* and one of them had *no*, and they were used to answer questions about whether to do a certain thing or not.[20] The practice is understood to be pre-Islamic and makes me think of the predynastic Egyptian Goddess Neith, whose "coat of arms" (two crossed arrows in front of an ankh) is found on a stela naming the female ruler of the First Dynasty in Egypt (around 3100 B.C.E.). Her name was Neith-Hotep, and she is one of a number of unsung female pharaohs from the early period in Egypt when the dynasties were forming. Females in Egypt with any ruling power at all were always understood to be priestesses as well, so this could very well point to a divinatory form of "drawing lots," or obtaining yes-no answers, that dates to this early female lineage.

Consider then the Amazon women, who bred horses and founded great cities in Asia Minor during the Bronze Age (2000 B.C.E.), worshipped the Goddess Artemis, and whose signifier (like Egyptian Neith's) was the bow and arrows. We might easily link their arrow practice to the Cycladic islands, with their "dove shrines" and powerful oracular centers. The Amazons' other symbol, the double axe, also defines the two polarities of yin and yang, waxing and waning, which could be read as yes or no. The Amazon Queen Ephesia founded Ephesus (on the west coast of Turkey, practically a stone's throw from the islands of Lesbos and Samos) in 2000 B.C.E., according to Turkish tour guides at that site today. There in later classical times the great Temple of Artemis of Ephesus was known as one of the Seven Wonders of the World. Statues of "Artemis of the Thousand Breasts" reproduced by the Romans can still be seen in the museum at the site. Pilgrims came from all over the ancient world to bring their offerings and ask their questions of the priestesses there. The popular mass rites of this widespread "mystery religion" were practiced by large groups of the populace for hundreds of years, and Artemis almost certainly functioned as a precursor of the Virgin Mary. (There is a small house near the site that is said to be the place where Mary lived as an old woman and died.) Remember that Paul's sermons to the Ephesians included constant reprimands to the women for considering themselves equal to men and speaking out in church.

Amazon tribes from the later classical period (around fifth century B.C.E.) had a widespread influence over all of Turkey and Central Asia, into Greece, Italy, and Celtic Europe, if we assume that the pervasive images of them are in any way accurate. Cimmerians, Scythians, Sauromatians, and Sarmations were all connected to tales of women hunters and warriors, who dressed like men and used battle-axes and bows and arrows. These same warrior women were often priestesses, as proven by burials excavated from around the Black Sea, and between the Don and Volga Rivers, in southern Russia by archaeologists today.

As part of a small expedition in 1997, led by archaeologists Jeannine Davis-Kimball and Russian Maria Ozir-Goreyaeva, I was privileged to visit museum archives of materials from these burials and see for myself the awesome remains of the Sauromatian warrior-priestesses with the bronze mirrors and arrowheads among their other so-called cultic belongings (altars, incense pots, bone spoons, white gypsum). Given the scholarly research on nomadic peoples from other areas, it's perhaps not too much of a long shot to imagine that Amazon women knew how to "cast lots," using their arrows for divination.

The Amazons (described as wearing mirrors on their belts) were crazy about their horses, and according to the histories, were understood to be excellent riders and horse breeders. Surely Demeter as "Mare Goddess" relates to their influence during what has been dubbed the "Orientalizing period" in Greek and Mediterranean culture. The term "Amazon" can be expanded to include all "barbarian" (foreign) women, from the perspective of the classical Greek writers, because they rode horses, hunted, and generally participated equally in life in a way that was considered strictly "male" in Greece. There are widespread images of Greeks fighting Amazons dressed in Persian trousers, Gorgons dressed like Amazons, maenads (Dionysian priestesses) riding horses, and warrior goddesses wearing Amazon outfits and carrying Gorgon shields.

It is interesting that much later, in the Middle Ages, a pagan Slav people on the south Baltic coast still practiced an interesting form of divination using a white or a black horse considered sacred to their deity. Laying spears on the ground, they would watch to see which foot the horse used first when stepping over the spears, whether the horse's hooves touched them, and so on. "Consultation by lots sometimes preceded this ceremony."[21] And the Nordic *Volva* (soothsayer and seer) from around the same time was oracular in a cultural context that included Valkyries, those warrior-women suspiciously similar to the Amazons of earlier times. The Valkyries' miraculous ability to fly through the air is probably related to the psychotropic herbal oracular practices of other pagan women (of the European Iron Age and into the Middle Ages) who danced in the sacred groves and rode through the air on their brooms; witches'-broom is one of many medicinal herbs still growing in Europe.

In Tibetan Buddhism, it is the dakinis, called "sky-goers" or "sky-maidens" (modern Valkyries?) who express the existence of "an underlying world order, embracing both natural and supernatural realities."[22] The dakinis are considered to be present whenever synchronicities and other supernatural epiphanies take place, but they are also known to incarnate as human women. A contemporary American woman, Tsultrim Allione, who became a Tibetan nun at the age of twenty and then gave back her vows so as to marry and have children, now teaches and "transmits" dakini practices that come from a female-founded lineage of such teachings and practices among Tibetan Buddhists.[23] Tibetan *tra* still perform their divination with mirrors and arrows, invoking the wrathful female deity Mahakali (divine protectress) to perform such divination as discovering the whereabouts of the present incarnation of the Dalai Lama.[24] The female *tra* are still called "mirror women,"[25] hearkening to an Asian female oracular tradition corroborated by priestess burials excavated in Russia and China.[26]

THE MOTHERPEACE YES-NO READING

When you sit down with your Motherpeace cards to ask a yes-no question, perhaps you can meditate on these earlier traditions of "casting lots" and making divinatory decisions that seem to be so much a part of women's history and female religious traditions. Imagine yourself in a long line of priestesses and official "Oracles" who could enter a trance state and provide the much-needed answers to questions for people who put their trust in them. Perhaps you want to take up yogic practices, like the yoginis and dakinis, that will help to develop your capacity to enter trance and visionary states, so that you can become more skillful in your pronouncements, and more insightful in your interpretations. In this way you can be clearer when you sit down to ask the cards a question that is for yourself or someone else.

As always, set the ritual scene with candles, incense, and a nice place to lay the cards out, and then center yourself with silent meditation, contemplating your question. The reading will be as clear as your focus, so the more exact you are able to be in phrasing your question, the better. When you ask the cards a yes-no question, you are essentially asking if it is in your interest to do one thing instead of another. In other words, you are not asking "should I" in the sense of some power outside of yourself giving you the answer and taking responsibility for it. You are asking your more holistic "inner mind" to speak to you, giving you a choice that has been made by your "higher self," with the understanding that your "higher self" has more information than your limited ego or "conditioned self."

Imagine that there is a part of you that knows everything, that is tuned in or in touch with all that is—a broader intelligence that includes the intuition, instincts, telepathy, extrasensory perception, and other psychic sensitivities, in addition to your ordinary, rational mind. This part of you has all the facts, as it were, and can make a decision that takes into consideration every salient point. It's hard to imagine, but we actually know everything in the past, present, and future at this moment in time. It's just a matter of being able to tune into our "subtle bodies" and utilize the information in a meaningful way.

To get in the best "head space" for doing this reading, it helps to really trust that some part of you already knows the answer, has all the details, and can help your conscious self make the absolutely correct, best decision for yourself. You really must suspend disbelief and be at peace in advance with whatever the answer is going to be. The reason I stress this essential state of surrender is that with this kind of formula, you can sometimes affect the cards by your will. So if you attempt to "will" the cards into the answer you think you want, you could end up with a confused reading that you can't understand.

METHOD

When you have shuffled the cards to your satisfaction, cut them once in the center and begin to count them out in three piles in front of you. You count each pile to thirteen, the magical number of lunar cycles in a year, sacred to women in the Old Religion of the Goddess as far back as the Venus of Laussel (30,000 B.C.E.) with her crescent horn notched thirteen times. It is no accident that women's magical menstrual number, thirteen, was demonized by Christianity and made into such an "evil" (or nowadays "unlucky") number that modern hotels don't even have a thirteenth floor. In this reading layout, we consciously take our number back.

The exception to the number thirteen is that in each pile, whenever you turn over an ace, you stop counting and leave the ace facing up instead of continuing to thirteen. There are four aces (Discs, Cups, Wands, Swords), and each one represents an influx of the energy of that particular element (earth, water, fire, air). Aces are always perceived in the tarot as "gifts," since they are the fresh, new beginning of the suit and signal the arrival of something new and exciting into your life. In the yes-no reading, the aces mean "yes" if they are turned upright, "no" if they are upside down, and "maybe" if they are exactly tilted to either side.

The strongest "yes" reading you can get is three aces right side up; the clearest "no" is three aces reversed; and the clearest "maybe" is when you get aces, but they are all sideways, neither up nor down.

But the cards are not always so cut and dried, and often your reading will be a mixture of aces and other cards, some of them up, some down, and you will have to figure out what you think it is telling you. That's why your focus is so crucial. The stronger and clearer your focus on the question, the clearer the answer is likely to be. The more vague your question, the more confusing the answer will be for you to read.

Let's take an example. What if you wanted to know whether you should move to another town. There are an amazing number of variables involved in such a question. The timing needs to be brought into focus: are you thinking of moving to another town next week, in a year, or just someday? And the purpose is important: are you wanting to move to a specific place for a specific reason, or do you just have the urge to go somewhere else? Bring your thoughts on the subject into focus, honing the question to a more and more precise place. You can do this by using the cards in a general way first, pulling cards at random to answer certain questions that help to narrow the subject.

Finally you formulate your question, after having considered it from all different directions. Rather than asking, shall I move? Ask, shall I move to such-and-such a town? If you know a precise time, add that: shall I move to such-and-such within three months? If there is a job waiting or a position to be filled or something specific that calls you, include that in the question: shall I move to such-and-such within three months in order to start teaching at the college there? So you throw the cards and get your three piles, which look like this: Ace of Wands upright, Ace of Cups upright, and Ace of Discs upright. This is the simplest, clearest answer possible—a definite yes! without any confusion. If the three aces were reversed, it would be the same kind of definite answer, but no. I always feel exhilarated with this kind of unambiguous response!

But let's say you get the following cards, which is certainly typical: Ace of Wands upright, Ace of Cups reversed, and 8 Swords upright. What does it mean? The Ace of Wands is clearly a yes, the Ace of Cups clearly a no, and the 8 Swords kind of threatening, with that person breaking Swords against the brick wall.

So how do you read it? Now is when you bring some of what you know from past readings to bear on the question. You treat the three cards as you would a "past, present, and future" reading (see chapter 4). The Ace of Wands is in the past position, telling us that you felt a strong impulse in the recent past to move to another town. But now in the present, with the Ace of Cups reversed, it seems like you have some emotional fears about the move, or perhaps someone you love doesn't want to move with you. In the future, the 8 Swords tells us you are going to experience a blockage

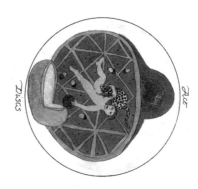

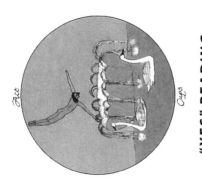

"YES" READING

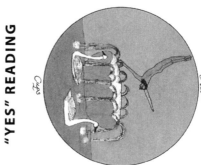

"NO" READING

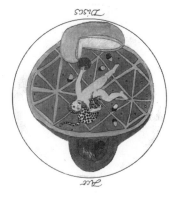

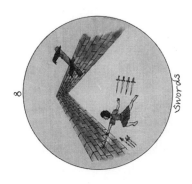

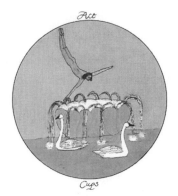

MAYBE READING

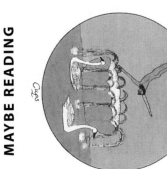

MIXED READING

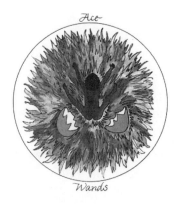

of some kind around this question. But the 8 Swords is only an illusion of an obstacle—it's not really real but is something thrown up by the mind as a defense against fear. Either you can process this yourself and figure out the answer, or you can wait until you become clearer about some of these details, and then ask again.

The past-present-future technique of reading the three cards is always helpful in this reading layout. Sometimes you will get three piles of thirteen cards each and no aces at all. This usually means you haven't asked the right question, or you haven't come close to focusing the question in such a way that it can be answered by either yes or no. You can still read the three cards as past-present-future and get some information, which may help you to zero in on your question, so that you can ask again and get aces. One ace is a weak answer, suggesting yes or no, but I wouldn't consider it binding. Two aces is stronger, showing a pretty strong tendency in that direction, especially when the two aces point in the same direction. Three aces is usually obvious, but if they all point in different directions, then you'll have to use past-present-future to decipher.

The aces themselves have a hierarchy of importance in the sense of being more or less tangible and "real." The Ace of Swords is really just an idea, so it could change in a moment. If it's your only ace upright, it means you think you want to do that, but it's not clear you'll be able to hold the thought long enough to manifest it. Ace of Wands is also very quick, like an intuitive grasp of something, or like passion, and it may or may not last, depending on the other cards (especially other aces). Ace of Cups is more real, one step closer to the "reality" of the physical plane. Just as scientists tell us that if we dream we are jogging it actually causes our pulse and heart rate to speed up, so the "dreambody" is where we practice for life, "clothing" our desires in form through our wanting. The Ace of Discs is a sure thing, a fait accompli, a done deal.

Using this hierarchy to look at the reading, you can see that if an ace falls in the past position and the other cards are not aces, the reading is very weak. If the ace falls in the center, present position, it's slightly stronger, and if it is an Ace of Discs it is fairly certain, even if the other cards are not aces. Any ace in the future is strong, because it's the way you are going to feel or act soon, so the answer is likely to be based on that ace. If the Ace of Discs is in the present along with any other ace in the past or future, then it's almost certain to happen, and the answer is yes. In fact, anytime there are two aces and one of them is the Ace of Discs upright, it is probably yes. But you will have to determine for yourself from the other cards if this is so in individual cases.

SUMMARY

To summarize, three aces up is the strongest answer, meaning absolutely yes; three aces down is equally strong in a negative direction, saying definitely not; and aces exactly turned to either side tell you maybe.

Anything else must be interpreted by you—the divinatory priestess—weighing all the various components and making a decision about what the cards are telling you. It's not quite as straightforward as throwing the dice, but it gives you ample opportunity to become aware of the many variables in most situations where you are having difficulty making a decision, and to work through some of the more challenging obstacles while you're at it.

CHAPTER EIGHT

MOTHERPEACE
AND THE
SACRED HOLIDAYS

I HAVE OFTEN WRITTEN ABOUT THE sacred holidays, those eight points of power in the cycle of seasons that define a calendar year: Winter Solstice, Candlemas, Spring Equinox, Beltane (May Day), Summer Solstice, Lammas, Fall Equinox, and Hallowe'en (All Hallow's Eve). These magical eight points on the circle of the year mark times when the relationships between the Sun, Moon, and Earth are particularly powerful and can be felt or experienced by us most profoundly. At these times, as I have described in other places, whether people are conscious of the holiday or not, we all have stronger experiences, bigger dreams, and more intense impressions of the invisible energies and forces. In other words, the holidays exist whether we recognize them or not.

The Sacred Calendar is a visible image superimposed over the invisible structure that holds reality in place in our world. Marking the eight magical spots on the calendar year and celebrating them in some way is part of the Old Religion of the Goddess, which is active again today in the Women's Spirituality movement.[27] These are the witches' "high holidays," and are recognized and honored in addition to the monthly New Moon and the Full Moon. The Solstices and Equinoxes are noted in our modern calendars as the beginning days of winter, spring, summer, and fall; and the "cross-quarter" days that fall in between them are claimed by Christianity and also included on the Julian calendar as church (and sometimes public) holidays.

I remember how shocked I was when my Catholic friends described contemporary rituals of crossing candles over your throat on Candle-Mass and the crowning of the May Queen in the Catholic schools and churches on Beltane (May Day). I myself remember celebrating "May Basket Day" as a child, when we delivered handmade baskets of goodies to our friends around the neighborhood. Anyone who has ever been to a state fair in August was participating in a modern version of Lammas, when the first fruits were brought to share at community celebrations. My special son Aaron Eagle is crazy about Hallowe'en, planning his costume weeks—even months—in advance. And, of course, in Latin countries the Day of the Dead is still honored by visiting cemeteries, putting out "suppers" for the dead, and honoring the *festivo* day with community rituals.

KEEPING THE HOLIDAYS

A profound way of tuning into the powers and practices of the worldwide culture of the Mother Goddess is to honor her ancient calendar of eight magical sacred holidays. It is not really necessary to "do ritual" on the sacred holidays, since if you simply make the space in your life to observe and pay attention, the holidays will "do" you. Tuning into the "play of the dakinis" will allow them to spontaneously appear in your life as synchronicities and supernatural events, which tend to take place at a higher frequency around the holidays.

In the following descriptions of the seasonal cycle of the year and the eight holidays, the particular unfolding I describe is applicable only to the northern hemisphere. In the south it will be the opposite, and near the equator, the seasons do not really unfold in a sequence of four climatic events, but rather alternate back and forth between two seasons—rainy and dry. I learned this lesson the hard way when I was invited to do a Hallowe'en (or Hallomas) ritual in Santiago, Chile, at the usual time in late October, before All Saints' Day and the Day of the Dead, which are honored in all the Latin countries on November 1 and 2. I was preparing for the ritual and happened to be walking in the country, where I noticed the honeysuckle blooming. It stopped me dead in my tracks. Here we were, preparing a ritual to celebrate the "dying" of the year and the time of honoring the dead, and it was spring! I brought this to the attention of my sponsors, and I modified the Hallowe'en ritual to accommodate this fact. Clearly, the indigenous earth-based tradition had been preempted by the Spanish colonization hundreds of years ago, and the people had been celebrating their religious holidays ever since then according to the seasonal cycle in Spain. Some Mapuche Indian women present at the ritual told me afterward that in their ceremonies, they keep the cycle of holidays in time with the seasons as they experience them, as I had urged for that strange Hallomas ritual.

WINTER SOLSTICE

At the moment of Winter Solstice, around December 21 each year, we experience the longest night and the shortest day of the year. At this apex of darkness, the world sleeps and the subterranean powers rule. In nothern climates, snow covers the ground and the air is freezing, forcing us indoors to light fires (now furnaces) and get the houses warm against the elements. We get up in the dark of morning, and by late afternoon, it is dark again. We need more sleep because we don't get enough sunshine and more vitamins because we lack the necessary nutrients that come from the fresh fruits and vegetables of summer. Most of us have less energy during the winter months, and sickness is rampant during these times. Colds and flu are endemic, as the germs get stronger in relation to the general weakening of our immune systems.

It used to be that communities would have been attuned to these darker, slower energies of winter. Without electric lighting, we would have had to yield to the demands of the long, cold winter nights. People in ancient and tribal cultures sat around the fire and told stories during the winter, passing on their beliefs in narrative forms, in what we have come to call oral tradition. The Winter Solstice holiday is the deepest and quietest of the eight holy days during the year, calling us down inside, to face the darkness and listen in the powerful emptiness. At this holiest of times, a "seed" is planted in us and in the world, and in the moment of the greatest darkness, the light begins again.

"Light is returning, even though this is the darkest hour, no one can hold back the dawn. Let's keep it burning, let's keep the light of hope alive. Make safe our journey through the storm," so goes a contemporary chant by Charlie Murphy.[28] Rituals for the Winter Solstice are designed to honor and appreciate the darkness, to welcome back the light that always miraculously returns, and to participate in the seeding of the New Year. It's a time for making wishes, for seeking a vision, and for making yourself available to receive the seeds and visions that are being planted in humanity with each new turning of the wheel of the year.

The Cards

Motherpeace images that pertain to this sacred time of year would include the quintessential Crone, Hecate herself, the queen of the night. You could also meditate on the Daughter of Discs on her winter vision quest, the Priestess of Swords in her snowy environment, or the 4 Discs—a woman closing the door of her hut in order to keep the wind off the hearth fire.

The Devil card is connected with the "negative Capricorn" energies and could represent the depression and gloom that overtake many people at the Winter Solstice season. More people die during this time than any other, and many are suicides.

The Moon card similarly depicts the "dark night of the soul" and the feeling of being fogged in or unable to see clearly; the suggestion in the card is to allow the intuition and the instincts to lead the way through the dark night. The Ace of Discs shows the charm of being inside near the warm fire on a cozy rug; 8 Cups might reflect the inner emotional darkness felt at this time; Son of Cups demonstrates a positive method of navigating the dark times, through meditation and the cultivation of inner stillness; 2 Wands depicts the visitations possible to those who become quiet and watchful; 3 Wands suggests creative activities that might be performed inside the "cave" of your home during the wintertime; 9 Wands shows a yogini practicing her winter art of raising the kundalini power for enlightened conscious awareness; Shaman of Wands implies a philosophical mentality that awakens in the dead of winter from time spent in reflection; Ace of Swords could be the decision to "turn over a new leaf" that so many of us express through New Year's resolutions; 9 Swords shows the nightmares that overtake some of us at times of darkness.

The Ritual: A Seed Is Planted in You

To practice a ritual with the Motherpeace cards on Winter Solstice, have ready a candle and matches, your deck of cards, and a journal for writing or drawing. Set up a place for yourself to be alone for a period of time, and when you're ready, turn out all the lights and sit quietly in the darkness for at least five minutes, longer if you can. Let the year that is ending pass by in your imagination, and reclaim with your mind the highlights and memorable moments, which you can distill into seed form on this darkest night of the year. When you have remembered what you can of the year, imagine that the rest is like compost on the ground for next year's garden, and throw it away, release it into the darkness. Consciously let go of any pain or sorrow left from the year, as well as anger, resentment, and feelings of futility.

When you are ready, light your candle and imagine that a similar light is being lit within you. Sit very still and meditate on the flame for five minutes, longer if you like. What is your destiny in this year? What seeds are you planting? What do you want/ wish/hope for in this coming year? What seeds or visions are *being* planted in you? When you are ready, write or draw any visions, hints, or predictions you received about the coming year. Choose a Motherpeace card to reflect this time, and a second one to predict your future. Write about the cards in your journal.

CANDLEMAS OR BRIGID'S EVE: FEBRUARY 1

Candlemas is the "Witches' Initiation" that I wrote about in chapter one, when I experienced my first conscious raising of the kundalini and heard a voice say, "I am one with all witches through all time." Six weeks after the Winter Solstice and six weeks before the Spring Equinox, this sacred holiday belonged to the Celtic Brigid, who was said to pass in the night and bestow healing power on any of her worshippers who left a silk scarf hanging out the window. The scarf could be used during the year to "doctor" anybody in the family who became ill. It is traditionally the time when Wiccan covens take in new members. Wicca is the name of the contemporary tradition that comes from European "witchcraft."

"Who were the Witches, where do they come from? Maybe your great-great-grandmother was one," goes the contemporary tune by Bonnie Bramble that is sung in women's groups around America.[29] The root word *wic* means "wise" according to some scholars, and "to bend" according to others, meaning essentially, "the wisdom to bend energy to your will," as witches are known to be able to do. "Witches were wise, wise women they say/And there's a little witch in every woman today!" In the Western magical tradition, the motto for practitioners of witchcraft is, "Do what thou wilt and harm none."

Candlemas is the time of the "quickening" of the energy of the new year, when the life force is beginning to return and the seed sprouts. The Hopi literalize this holiday by sprouting seeds in the kivas, and some traditions say that the snakes come up above the ground at this time. I like to link this metaphorically to the female "snake-power" or kundalini energy, recognizing that as the life force returns with the longer hours of daylight and sunshine, our sexuality and healing energies begin to become enlivened. We start to hope for spring, and indeed this holiday in America is called Groundhog Day and has as its prophetic legacy the groundhog, seeing its shadow or not, and thereby determining whether we will have an early or a late spring.

The Cards

Motherpeace cards attuned to this holiday are, first and foremost, the Strength card, which is an image of the red-haired Irish Brigid on her fairy mound with her shamanic animal helpers and the "heat that heals" coming out of her left hand. The Star is another image that relates to the influx of electrical energies represented by the astrological sign of Aquarius that rules this holiday.

Strength

High Priestess shows the inner mind awake and alert to every unfolding message; and the Shaman of Swords depicts the spontaneous expression of these energies in oracular speech.

The Fool could show the unpredictability of events during this holiday, and the Tower suggests the radical change or "paradigm shift" that comes with any bona fide initiation.

The 2 Discs might indicate the in-between feeling of Candlemas, not really dark but still not light; 9 Discs shows the solitary creativity of winter-into-spring; 2 Cups could express the quickening of a sexual promise; 7 Cups shows the choices beginning to be felt as spring approaches; Priestess of Cups expresses the longing for love that often comes over us as winter recedes; 8 Wands depicts that the energies have begun to move again; Ace of Swords is the awakened intention, perhaps achieved through chanting a mantra in meditation.

The Ritual: Healing and Purification Scarf

On February 1 (Candlemas Eve), find an old silk scarf from your drawers or purchase one from a secondhand store, and bring it to your ritual. If possible, acquire some self-lighting charcoal (the kind they use in the Catholic church) probably from a New Age bookshop, plus incense resins for burning on the charcoal (such as copal from Central America, or frankincense and myrrh from North Africa). Have the Motherpeace cards ready, along with any icons or images that feel sacred to you—a snake would be appropriate. When you are ready, light candles and light your charcoal. Be sure you have a container for it that can tolerate very high heat, such as a piece of high-fired pottery, or an incense burner designed for this purpose. I use a metal cauldron on three legs with a handle that reminds me of a witch's cauldron. After a few minutes, the charcoal will begin to turn white, at which time you can begin to drop small pieces of incense resin on it. (If you add the resins before the fire is hot enough, the resins will put out the charcoal.)

The intense smoke that generates from this form of burning incense is very powerful at opening your psychic senses, cleansing your space of any negative energies or obstacles, and putting you in an "altered" state of consciousness. Be sure you have some ventilation or a big enough room to handle the smoke, and don't get it too close to any smoke alarms! You can carry the smudge around the house to cleanse and purify every room and all your special objects. Finally, put the scarf through the smoke three times to consecrate it to Brigid and the healing goddesses. Then drape it out of one of your windows for the night, in order that it can "pick up" the vibrations of the holiday as Brigid passes in the night. Choose a Motherpeace card before you go to bed, and in the morning, bring the scarf in and wrap it around your cards if you like, or put it somewhere special so you'll have it when you need it for healing. (You can wrap it around your neck if you're getting a sore throat, and so forth.)

SPRING EQUINOX

"Equal-night" is the literal meaning of this holiday, when the day and night are precisely the same length, and when an egg will balance on its end. Each spring for twenty-three years now, Urban Shaman Donna Henes, author of *Celestially Auspicious Occasions,* has performed a public "Eggs Standing on End Ceremony" at the World Trade Center Plaza in New York City, where she invites you to bring your own drum or percussion instrument and join the fun.[30] On or near March 20, the Spring Equinox happens when the sun moves into the fire sign of Aries, and spring officially begins. By this time, the days are getting noticeably longer and the sun is out more, so our energy has begun to return. Depending on where you live, the winter storms are receding and the buds are beginning to appear on the trees. In northern California, where I live, that all happens much earlier, and by Spring Equinox everything is green and fruit trees are in flower. It is definitely a time of celebration for the return of spring.

The "rites of spring" bring to mind sexuality and the bursting into bloom of our life force energies. The thrill of spring is that somehow, having survived the winter's slow, dark, sometimes depressing qualities, the wheel makes its inevitable turn and brings back around the sunshine, and the romance and happiness we associate with it. Persephone returns, and her mother, Demeter, brings the earth back to life in honor of the return of her daughter from the Underworld. The days begin to lengthen now, during this period daylight savings time kicks in, and those of us in winter climates can go out into nature again.

In many parts of the world, ancient women left their houses and escaped into the forests and the mountains, where they celebrated the rites of Dionysus in the strict company of other women. These "orgiastic" rituals involved using the tambourine or frame drum, ecstatic dancing, and drinking inebriating herbal concoctions that facilitated spirit flight and trance journeys to other dimensions. As late as the Middle Ages, reports were made about groups of wild women dancing in the Carpathian Mountains of Hungary, and the mountains of Thessaly in northern Greece, the site of the earlier Neolithic (Sesklo and Dimini) cultures that worshipped the Goddess in the sixth and fifth millennia B.C.E.

The Cards

The epitome of springtime is the Magician, that "just do it" character of this Major Arcanum whose every impulse is channeled into assertive leadership, powerful manifestation, and inspired self-expression. Karen Vogel modeled this image after punk rocker Patti Smith, whose revolutionary approach to musical self-expression in the 1970s pioneered a whole new genre of music in the West. Ace of Wands shows the new self bursting out of the egg—a joyous rebirth; the Daughter of Wands represents Persephone herself rushing from her winter cave, and with the help of her imaginary friend, the unicorn, actively turning the wheel of the year.

Magician

The 3 Cups depicts a Dionysian ritual, and 6 Cups the wave of ecstasy that carries us into abandonment of our usual senses; both cards include images of fantasy creatures as well.

The 3 Swords could be an image of the romantic triangles that constellate with the coming of spring, and 6 Swords could be women getting out of their physical bodies—and out of their patterned routines—by using "flying ointment" at one of their nocturnal forest rituals.

The Ritual: Motherpeace Tree Reading

For your Spring Equinox ritual, go outdoors. Find a place in the woods or on a mountainside, where you can imagine ancient people communing with nature—before electricity, automobiles, and airplane travel became the norm. Find a tree that especially appeals to you, and sit near or under it, letting your roots go down to join with the roots of the tree. Let yourself merge with the mind of the tree, and let your body sink into an experience of oneness with the earth. Spend at least ten minutes in silence, during which you establish a rapport or telepathic contact with the consciousness of the tree. (To do this, you may have to get over feeling silly, but force yourself to suspend your ordinary critical judgment, and just for a few minutes, let yourself be childlike.)

When you're ready, take out your Motherpeace cards and lay them out in a circle in front of you on the ground, facedown. Do a vertical reading of your (1) roots (grounding), (2) trunk (stability), (3) branches (outreach), and (4) leaves (communication), and measure your current well-being against the structure of the tree. Where are you strongest? Weakest? Where could you use a little work, and what would be helpful for clearing or healing? (For this question, you might like to draw a helper card.) Breathe in the fresh powers of nature in the spring, all the way down to your roots, and then ask a friend to go dancing!

BELTANE OR MAY EVE: MAY 1

It's the Beltane bonfires that the pagans used to jump over in celebration of the power of the fire inside us. The Taurus time of year is about exalting the senses, connecting with sexuality through dance and lovemaking. This was the legendary time of the rising of the sap, and young people in Britain ran naked and made love in the corn furrows on Beltane Eve even into the twentieth century. In ancient agricultural times, such activity worked as "sympathetic magic" for the whole community, spreading energy and vibration over the crops like fertilizer, bringing harmony and abundance to the land and all the living creatures.

The Maypole dance—a ritual only for children now—is an unveiled symbolic tribute to the raised phallus of Pan, the "goat-god" consort of Diana-Aradia, Queen of the Witches. The May baskets we delivered to each other as kids in Iowa during the 1950s were filled with romantic hints and yummy things to stimulate the taste buds, the olfactory nerves, and the visual senses. The crowning of the May queen hearkens back to a time when the High Priestess and her chosen consort would lead the way into the woods for enactment of the "Great Rite" or Sacred Marriage.

In Mexico, the peasants chose to declare their independence around Beltane, on May 5. In California, where so many Spanish-speaking people live, we celebrate Cinco de Mayo every year with parades and parties in the streets. In many places around the world, May 1 is a workers' holiday. One of the best Beltane rituals I remember happened out in the country in northern Arizona, when the women and children strung flowers for our hair and paraded through flower-covered arches that we created together. Beltane— when the honeysuckle blooms—teaches us about children, the faery realm and the "little people," and the magical energies of love, sensuality, and fertility.

The Cards

The Empress is the classical ruler of Beltane, with her awakened physical sensuality and nurturing relatedness; she is Mother Nature incarnate. The images in the background delineate the "storied tradition" of our ancestors, from the Venus of Laussel, to the throned Artemis of Catalhöyük, to Demeter-Ceres and the transformation mysteries of the grain (agriculture). In her yoga for the body and meditation for the mind, the Priestess of Discs depicts a maternal garden of delights.

The Shaman of Discs shows the mature and more material side of Taurus—the one who can make money and work hard on the physical plane. The 7 Discs shows us how to sustain the physical gestation of pregnancy or a garden, 10 Discs represents the successful birth in a circle of community support, and 9 Cups is the "wishing card" that gets you what you want in the world.

The 4 Wands is a Beltane ritual par excellence, and 5 Wands begins the summer games; the Son of Wands could be sacred Pan himself, dancing his desires in the persona of the sacred Clown. Even the Hierophant (V) goes back to pre-Christian times, as the priest who presided over the "hieros gamos" or sacred marriage of the priestess with the king whose coronation she was empowering through her bloodline.

The Ritual: Children Plant Seeds

A ritual for Beltane might include plants and children. Gather the neighborhood children together in your backyard or at a nearby park, and have small pots for planting ready. Let them choose seeds from a selection you've prepared in advance that includes interesting varicol-ored beans and kernels of corn that will sprout and grow quickly, demonstrating to the children the power of the life force as the sum-mer nears. Have potting soil and water ready, so they can plant and water their own seeds and take the pots home. Give them very sim-ple instructions for growing the plants, and suggest they have a par-ent help them transplant them into the ground at the proper time.

Have the children come to the ritual dressed as fairies and elves, and get them to discuss the "little people" who help with the plants that grow. If this is a stretch for your belief system, why not read ahead of time something from the Findhorn, Scotland, exper-iment, such as Dorothy MacLean's wonderful book about listening to the spirits who help with the plants.[31] Or tell them about how the Hopi sing to their corn seeds and to the plants once they're in the ground. Let each child pick a card from the Motherpeace deck and "read" them for each other. Encourage them to use their "guessing" minds and not to be afraid to say what they think.

SUMMER SOLSTICE

Summer Solstice falls on or near June 20, when the sun moves out of Gemini and into the sign of Cancer. It signals the longest day and the shortest night, and it usually coincides with our furthest extension of energy. Paradoxically, at exactly the moment we expe-rience the maximum daylight, the nights will begin to grow longer and the light begins to dwindle. There is death in life, night in day, and always the yin is contained within the yang (and vice versa). There is a poignant quality to the long summer evenings, some-thing bittersweet that pulls from under the high energy.

Ancient people in the southwestern United States who lived at Chaco Canyon placed giant rocks high on a mesa that caught a single ray of sun on the morning of Summer Solstice and brought it precisely down into a spiral they had carved on a rock. This "Sun Dagger" (as archaeologists called it) went into the center of the spiral and out again, all in the course of a few minutes, creating an astronomical miracle. Other earth-based people all over the planet expressed and honored the Summer Solstice in similar ways to celebrate and mark the sun's most powerful point in the yearly cycle. A woman archaeologist, who serendipitously arrived on the scene and "discovered" this amazing and magical happening, found that it took several years to convince the academic establishment it was authentic.

At this time of year, the days are endless, our energies are abundant, and many of us feel invincible and ready for anything. For the children (and teachers) school is out, and it's time to relax. Families take vacations, have barbecues in the backyard; kids go swimming every day, ride bikes, play ball, explore the woods and parks. At best, we all experience a quality of utmost expansion in our lives. It's hot out, which can be exhausting, and suddenly there are all kinds of bugs around. Various kinds of berries begin to ripen and become available, and fresh fruits and vegetables in general begin to enliven our tables. No matter what our actual situation, summer generally brings a feeling of freedom and liberation that often begs to be expressed through our bodies.

The Cards

Summer Solstice is expressed by the Lovers and the Chariot cards, Gemini and Cancer, the "urge to merge" with all the stimuli in our environment, the myriad choices, and our ability to move into intentional action and activity on our own behalf. The Lovers depicts the conflict of having more than one interest, and the need to make choices; the Chariot shows the development of the independent ego who can cope with its own independence.

Chariot

Summer is also like the Wheel of Fortune, with activities and rewards arriving after a year of hard work, as if someone had given the wheel a spin and everything we'd been working for had begun to take shape in our lives.

The Son of Swords shows us how the hot summer sun can make us feel overextended and cranky or selfish, but the Daughter of Swords shows us how to raise the energy and get things done! The aridity of his totally mental approach to life is contrasted by the grounded addition of her animal instincts.

The Ace of Cups shows a plunge into relaxation and self-appreciation, 6 Discs suggests contact and connection, and 6 Wands depicts a burst of fiery creative passion channeled into spontaneous expression.

The Ritual: Hiking

Summer Solstice demands physical activity, so pack a picnic lunch and take a hike! Drop everything, leave your work and projects behind, and go into nature for a walk that you have always wanted to take. Depending on your physical abilities and your level of interest, you can go bird-watching, or backpack into a wilderness area, but get out there. Go with a friend, or take an opportunity to be by yourself, whichever is more relaxing and fun. As you walk, open yourself to this sacred time of year. Be aware of the heat and light, honor the sun in some way, either inwardly or with an outer gesture or intuitive ritual.

Perhaps you will arrive at your destination early enough to watch the sunrise on this special day, or stay late enough to see the sunset. Recent research has shown that even bears stop what they're doing and hike up a mountainside to watch in silent ecstasy as the sun sinks below the horizon.[32] When you find the right spot, you can bring out your Motherpeace cards and do a three-card reading for the Solstice as directed in chapter 3: a Major for the important energy of the day, a People card for yourself at this sacred time, and a Minor for the area of your life where this holiday will demonstrate itself.

LAMMAS OR AUGUST EVE: AUGUST 1

Ancient people tended to treat the entire landscape as the body of Mother Earth and seem to have universally invented processions and powwows—gatherings over her body to celebrate her fertility, and the awesome cycles of regenerative life they experienced within her being. Some of the earliest structures in the British Isles are henges, or great round circles shaped on the land, where people gathered together at annual fairs, to meet and marry, to share their produce and livestock, and to tell stories and exchange information and culture. Today our county and state fairs are the remnant of these ancient practices and still operate as places where prize-winning produce and livestock are displayed and teenagers win prizes. It's interesting that the Michigan Womyn's Music Festival—a gathering of thousands of women who come together to listen to music, take workshops, and share rituals of female spirituality together—has happened every August for more than twenty years.[33]

Michael Dames suggests that the Lammas holiday was cele-brated in England on Silbury Hill, that great mound of earth piled up to represent the pregnant belly of the Mother, who gave birth in a graphic visual demonstration on the Full Moon in August. The rising and cresting of the Moon over the mound would have created a shadow that moved over her belly and out, as if she were giving birth to the child who had grown through all the holidays since Winter Solstice.[34] Lammas is the time to share your creative endeavors for the year, to give expression to your poetry, songs, books, and births of various kinds—everything that has manifested since the Winter Solstice when the seeds were planted. It is the gathering in of "first fruits," a taste of what's to come in the fall harvest.

The Cards

Lammas time falls in the sign of Leo and is represented by the Emperor and the Sun cards. The Emperor shows us how to hold the energy long enough to manifest our desires through force of will, and the Sun shows us the playful, childlike Leo personality emerging through spontaneous, uninhibited, theatrical self-expression.

The Priestess of Wands, with her lion beside her, demonstrates the fiery will that goes straight after what it wants, confident in the presence of the healing "heat that heals." The 7 Wands shows us how to stand our ground when challenged and speak with the courage of our convictions, and 10 Wands shows that the summer energies have blown our circuits and we'd better figure out some way of releasing the energy—like dancing all night.

The Ritual: Gaming

Lammas is a "first fruits" festival, when you gather people together to share your abundance in an early thanksgiving ritual of praise for the creativity and fertility of the universe. Gather some friends together (or your women's group, or suggest a picnic at work) and set up yard or table games, "gamble" with cards or dice, and have a potluck with the central activity an ongoing Motherpeace game. Invite people who usually don't involve themselves with such things—the husbands of those in your women's group, for instance, or the families in your neighborhood. Make it fun, and take the taboo out of it. Dress like a gypsy and read fortunes, or have people play charades, using the cards for stimulating ideas. Use the power of the holiday to break through the usual resistances and enter new space together. When it's all done, give thanks in private at your altar and start planning next year's activity.

FALL EQUINOX

The Autumn Equinox happens on or around September 21, as the sun moves from Virgo (sign of the "Virgin") into Libra, and we begin to feel the pull of winter. The harvest begins and will last until the last fruits of the vine are picked and stored, and the force of the seasons challenges us to begin to gather ourselves in as well. The strong outer activities of summer must be surrendered now to a quieter, more introverted approach to life, or else we will begin to feel the ill effects in the area of our physical health of our own resistance. Yet September in the West is when school starts again, and the social season gets in full swing with organizational activities that will last until the winter holiday.

In ancient Greece, Fall Equinox marked the time of the Mysteries, when thousands of people came together at the site in Eleusis (not far from Athens) to celebrate Persephone's descent into the Underworld and the initiation it marked. The narrative tells us that Demeter, in her grief at losing her daughter to Hades, would withdraw the life force from the world of the living, causing everything to become barren while she ransacked the place, looking for a sign of her daughter.

Equinox, the time of "equal night" and equal day, warns us that it is time to find our personal balance in the cosmic scheme of things, and to begin our annual descent into a deeper communion with ourselves and the divine in nature. The abundance of fresh fruits and vegetables reminds us to use everything, waste nothing, and be thankful for all. From this knowledge came the processes of preparing food for storage that, until very recently, would have dominated the fall schedule of activities for our mothers and grandmothers. Drying fruits, canning vegetables, and putting up preserves wasn't just a quaint activity practiced by "primitive" people; it was an ancient form of survival based on living in right relation with the planet. "Thank you, Mother Earth, thank you, Sister Water; thank you for my birth, thank you from your daughter. Thank you, Brother Sun, thank you air in motion; thank you every one, earth, air, sun, and ocean."

The Cards

Justice is the Major Arcanum that best depicts the Fall Equinox, with the three Norns at the Tree of Fate demonstrating natural law and the action of karmic cause and effect. Like Inanna of ancient Sumer, we had best heed the "call of the Great Below" and begin to prepare for our descent. The Hanged One similarly demonstrates the surrender needed to truly "let go" of our ego identities and sink into the oblivion of the long (psychic) winter night. If we can begin to let go of outer activities and shift our focus to an alignment with our higher minds, the light within us will become radiant and will illuminate and purify our experience in the world, and we will be able to experience the Temperance—a dynamic and high-powered balance between extremes, walking the "middle way," powerful and centered at the same time.

Hanged One

Two Swords represents Libra's continuous effort at achieving balance in movement, 4 Swords the time-out needed to find your center and purify your chakras or energy centers, and 10 Cups the community in sacred ceremony together, giving thanks for the bountiful harvest and entering into a collective celebration. The 3 Discs shows women working together to build a structure for shelter that will last through the winter, and 8 Discs the hard daily work of staying on the path of nonresistance by attending to what's in front of you. The Son of Discs knows how to focus on tasks and keep his eye on the target ahead, planning and taking care of the myriad details involved in the harvesttime. If this is not done, the 7 Swords shows the inevitable outcome, a feeling of scarcity from unstable planning, or the obstruction of the 8 Swords that follows.

The Ritual: Making a Fetish Doll

For Fall Equinox, gather together some colorful fall fruits—either from your own garden, or from a farmers' market near your home—to make the centerpiece for your ritual. Then take a walk outdoors and pick up leaves, sticks, rocks, shells, feathers, bones, and anything else you find and gather all these found items together on a tray or table for the making of your fetish (an amulet or talisman in the shape of something you recognize from life). Even objects from modern civilization can be used in fetish making, such as copper wire, metal washers for faucets, and various gizmos and things you find on the street and in the garage. You should have one larger stick or bone as a "body" for the doll you are going to make, and some waxed linen or embroidery thread, scraps of leather or fabric, needles with large eyes, buttons, beads, and perhaps old pieces of jewelry or ornamentation.

When you're ready, put on a tape of Goddess chants or meditation music, settle yourself into a comfortable chair or an easy position on the floor, and let yourself begin to "see" the stick or bone as the body of an anthropomorphic figure. It may not be a person but might instead take shape as a snake, horse, deer, or some other creature. And it may stay abstract; just be open to whatever it "tells" you. Give yourself plenty of time for the creation of your fetish, so that you can figure out how to attach the various things you decide to put on it without using glue, paste, or tape (which are artificial/chemical). Be creative, be original, be improvisational. This is a dance and a dialogue between you and your shamanic work of art. As you bind it with thread and hang things on it, it will begin to direct and guide you in the process.

When you complete your project, pull a Motherpeace card to "read" the meaning of the holiday as well as to give you information about the magic that is contained in your fetish-doll. Burn sage to smudge yourself and your doll, and put the fetish somewhere you can see it every day, such as on an altar or your bedside table. It will continue to reveal its magic to you over the next few months.

ALL HALLOWS EVE: HALLOWE'EN

Hallowe'en falls on October 31 in the United States and is celebrated mainly by children all over the country, who outfit themselves in costumes representing old-fashioned ghosts, goblins, and monsters, or characters from the popular media such as Batman or Xena, the Warrior Princess. The trappings of this holiday come from old European customs, such as lighting pumpkins (jack-o'-lanterns) around the ritual circles in England so that people could find their way in the dark. Witches with broomsticks figured prominently in the Hallowe'en experience when I was young, as well as gypsies and fortune-tellers with crystal balls. Most of this tradition was eradicated in Europe during the Burning Times, yet it has somehow withstood the test of time in America by becoming a children's holiday.

When we let the children (dressed as "spooks") go door to door on Hallows Eve to trick-or-treat in their neighborhoods, we are acknowledging and participating in an ancient understanding that on this particular night, the veil between the worlds is particularly thin. The dead are believed to walk the land, and our communication with them is at its all-time best for the year. People give the children treats as part of an old tradition of this cross-quarter day that is linked to "Hecate's suppers," the giving of food to the ancestral ghosts in the cemeteries, or to the demons who haunt the crossroads where such dinners were laid on that night. This custom seems clearly related to Indian and Tibetan Buddhist Tantric feasts that are celebrated as *gana puja,* an invocation and food offering to the invisible guardians and spirits who protect and guide the living.

It is at Hallowe'en—All Hallows Eve—that divination reaches its most powerful level, and we are likely to experience big dreams or visions, powerful and intense energies, and a sense of altered consciousness of some kind. It was Hallowe'en night in 1979 when I dreamed one of my most powerful prophetic dreams:

that we were living too close to an active volcano. In the spring of 1980, Oregon's Mount Saint Helens erupted only a day's drive from my home.

The Cards

The classic image for Hallowe'en is, of course, the Death card with the leaves falling from the trees, the skeleton curled up in a fetal burial position, and the snake shedding its magical skin. The Death card tells us about reincarnation and the cycles of life that were recognized and worshiped by our ancient ancestors. The energies of Scorpio are depicted in the Shaman of Cups, with her face painted in white gypsum like priestesses of old, and the "cauldron of transformation," which she stirs over the alchemical fire like the Celtic Cerridwin or the African Circe.

Death

Daughter of Cups shows a lighter side to Scorpio, the humor and love of sensuality and sexual connection represented in this "hot" water sign. As the archetypal consort, she awaits a willing partner with whom to enter into a transformative experience. The 4 Cups shows someone who knows she needs to "cross over," to go deeper into the possibility of profound change. The Judgement shows the outcome of such a transformation, when the heart is opened and the healing energy pours through the human vessel and into the world. And the World card is another image of the shifting and changing forms that house the invisible energy that is always in motion, or the soul as it moves through incarnations.

The Ritual: Scrying

The old traditional ritual for celebrating Hallowe'en was to gaze into water or a mirror, called "scrying" by the European ancestors from whom we get much of the Western magical tradition. Crystal gazing is also part of this old method of practicing clairvoyance or second sight. Decide which method you would like to attempt (maybe all three) and gather the necessary equipment: a shiny mirror (could be modern glass, or obsidian, or shiny metal like those used by ancient nomadic people); a bowl of water; or a clear crystal ball on a stand.

To prepare for your ritual, why not create a supper for the dead ancestors by putting little servings of everything you are having for dinner on a special plate. Include beverages by pouring a little wine, beer, or mineral water on the plate, and light a stick of incense, which you stand up in the food. Take the entire plate outdoors after you've said a prayer over it. If you like, you could chant the Sanskrit syllables OM-AH-HUM over the plate for five minutes, and visualize all the dakinis and guardian spirits, as well as the ghosts of your ancestors, arriving at the sound of your vocal invitation, in order to partake of the magnificent feast you are offering them. After putting the plate outside, eat your own dinner in a state of gratitude and reverence.

Finally, lower the lights in the room (perhaps leave only a candle burning) and begin to stare gently into the bowl, the crystal, or the mirror. Relax your mind, so that you aren't tense or stiff, and allow your eyelids to fall to a soft focus that is not a fixed stare. Some soft music in the background may be helpful, or you might like to make sound yourself by shaking a rattle for five or ten minutes, or beating a steady drumbeat. In this way, you'll facilitate a trance state for yourself, which will enhance your ability to "see" into the mirror, and ultimately into other dimensions. Do this activity for as long as you like, without pressure to accomplish any particular goal. It will be very dreamy and impressionistic, and you may or may not see anything in a concrete way. Just let yourself enter into a reverie and receive the benefits of contact with the ancient ones. When you feel like it, choose Motherpeace cards to represent your past, present, and future, and reflect on them.

WINTER SOLSTICE: A YEAR AND A DAY LATER

Finally, the wheel brings us all the way around to the Winter Solstice again, in the initiatory period known as "a year and a day." If you have practiced the rituals suggested in this chapter, or others that you have improvised, for all the eight sacred holidays of the cycle, then you have officially initiated yourself into the Old Religion of the Goddess. Celebrate on Winter Solstice by giving yourself a piece of jewelry that represents your spiritual path and by taking a ritual bath with oils or salts while listening to a tape of some music. Debbie Collins developed a bath ritual for holidays that includes a Venus of Willendorf soap bar, a small jar filled with olive oil and a wick for lighting, and instructions for settling into the ritual tub and asking the Goddess to bless you for the coming year.

CHAPTER NINE

MOTHERPEACE
IN MODERN
LIFE

ALL OF THIS ORACULAR INFORMATION wouldn't matter very much if we couldn't find ways of using it in our everyday lives. Most modern (or perhaps I should say "postmodern") women today are busy and pressured by the challenges facing us at work and in our relationships, as well as those regarding child rearing and (perhaps most of all) how we can discover and liberate our personal creative expression. Since the late 1970s, when Karen Vogel and I made the Motherpeace cards, things in the world have changed a lot, and although some changes are for the better, many are not.

Karen and I with my two daughters were able to "drop out" of our culture in the 1970s to a certain extent and live on very little money while we chose to take significant time out (three years) from jobs or school to further our studies and delve into our creativity. Nowadays, this would not be possible in the same way, because the cost of living has risen astronomically since then.

When my young women students ask me today how to find the right livelihood, I advise them to do whatever they can to earn the rent, since without that stable base of support, you can't discover anything.

The globalization process that has been under way in the past two decades can seem very distant from the everyday issues of modern women. What multinational corporations are doing and thinking, the state of the international money economy and the stock exchange, even complicated trade agreements such as GATT and NAFTA can seem irrelevant to a young single mother, working as a secretary, who is depressed about her relationship life and is interested in learning about the Motherpeace tarot cards. If we live our lives in harmony with the earth, consciously and cooperatively, can we make the world a better place or as New Age thinking would have it, create our own better world?

Unfortunately the remote and anonymous transnational minds behind the global markets are making decisions that are affecting all of us every day, and in every way. Conditions in the world are bleeding into our psychic realities and affecting our health (physically and emotionally), as well as determining the concrete everyday state of our outer experience: whether we have jobs, how much money we earn, the taxes we pay, the state of the school systems our children are required to attend, the relative availability and quality of health care, public assistance, and access to things we take for granted, like the arts. If we only consider any one of dozens of environmental factors—the huge amount of toxic wastes dumped into rivers and water supplies, for example—it becomes clear that we are no longer able as individuals to control the basic realities of our own lives.

In the 1970s, many activists (feminists, leftists, civil rights workers, and environmentalists) devoted a good proportion of their energies to the development of conscious lifestyles that might take less from the earth and give back a certain amount. Our models for this kind of thinking were based on tribal and native populations who have managed to live in harmony with the planet, through approaches that have come to be called sustainable agriculture, forestry, city planning, and so on. Jerry Mander's excellent and inspiring work, *In the Absence of the Sacred,* is an example of this kind of thinking, where he discussed the marginalization and attempted assimilation of Native Americans, who want neither and who own their own sustainable ways of life as part of their long legacy on the North American continent. American society should be paying attention to and modeling itself after them, if we want to survive in the coming generations.

   An example of this thinking in action is how, for seven severe drought years in California, many of us basically stopped flushing our toilets. Enterprising environmentalists developed toilets that flush in more environmentally friendly ways and use less water, and so forth. Taking simple actions like this came to be promoted in books with names like *Fifty Ways to Save the Earth,* and such philosophies were integrated to some extent into schools and public education. All of this made us feel better and gave us a sense of participating in a community of people organized around environmental actions that would make a difference. A moral attitude developed alongside of this, naturally, that looked askance on anyone flushing their toilets or (Goddess-forbid) taking long showers.

   What a shock of sickening recognition I felt reading John Robbins's book, *Diet for a New America,* in which he documents (among many other atrocities of modern life) that *more than half* of all the water used in the United States is used by the meat industry in the process of making hamburgers. Having been a vegetarian since 1976, I felt it was a moment of absolute clarity and profound despair. It was a kind of epiphany that shone a bright light on the delusion under which I labored for all those years as I was being careful not to run the water while I brushed my teeth. As feminists have maintained without budging for twenty-five years, there (still) are no personal solutions: the personal is political.

This is not to suggest that we stop saving water, caring about endangered species, and working to create a better environment for ourselves and the coming generations. Every time any one of us acts even in small ways to make change happen, our positive intention vibrates out from us and makes a tangible difference in our world. Acts of healing toward the world heal us as well. Because each of us is like a single cell in the planetary body, and because all cells have consciousness, each of us has a link to the whole through our instincts, our emotions, and our visionary capacities. Whatever we can do to open ourselves to information from the invisible mind of nature furthers the goal of healing and transformation. And whatever steps we take to concretely make the world a better place not only changes the immediate external environment but also furthers our spiritual development.

The general purpose of this book (and the Motherpeace) is to guide women in making more informed decisions for ourselves in our daily lives, using our intuitions and instincts and whatever extrasensory perceptions we might be able to liberate for our own use. Certainly, in a society that is stacked against women and people of color, any tools we can acquire for better perceiving and meeting our own needs are important and useful. All the earlier chapters were devoted to helping women make use of the cards for solving personal dilemmas, and achieving some sense of harmony and self-awareness in the face of mounting external pressures. Personal meditation and spiritual practices help all of us to cope better with whatever way the conditions in our outer life happen to manifest.

This chapter will take a slightly broader view and suggest ways of perhaps changing the larger society in which you find yourself, by bringing some of your personal spiritual path (including the

Motherpeace cards) into public spheres where they may not always be welcome. In other words, I'd like to encourage you to take what you have learned and rock the boat a little. Without necessarily becoming a radical, you can still create ripples in the macrocosm which is, after all, having a daily (and often deadly) effect on the microcosmic world of your personal concerns.

I've often told my women students over the years that in order to become a "medicine woman" or a "woman of power" (both very popular ideas in the late 1980s and early 1990s), it is necessary also to become a feminist. With so much negative media attention, the *F*-word has gone out of favor, and most young, postmodern 1990s women demand to be liberated without calling it by that name. Yet by definition, for women to become either "liberated" or "empowered" in a male-dominated society is an anachronism and therefore has to be fought for in order to be— even slightly—attained. It is not given as a reward for right action or good behavior. As a woman, choosing to follow an autonomous spiritual calling means you will automatically be going against the grain of the larger culture, and any progress will demand that you assert yourself as you come up against the built-in obstacles designed to stop you.

Now it's very helpful for a woman to learn how to ground herself, becoming progressively more "real" to herself over time. There is a natural, organic process that begins to unfold for any woman who steps onto a path of self-authorization or spiritual autonomy, which Motherpeace certainly is. We gradually begin to experience ourselves at the center of our lives, rather than at the periphery. What matters to a woman becomes of central impor-tance to her as she becomes aware of herself and comes into direct contact with the stirrings of her soul. This is what the great women writers have expressed over the centuries, and why even certain novels from the eighteenth and nineteenth centuries still speak to modern women in women's studies courses around the country.

At the heart of this issue is the theme of "subjectivity," the perspective of whoever is at the center of the discourse that is taking place and whatever knowledge is being claimed. What has happened is that the white male perspective has been universalized and made to seem normal. Then, by definition, all other perspectives are "other"—foreign, alien, different, marginalized, estranged. To enter onto a spiritual path such as Motherpeace that organically brings you home to your center is going to disrupt the normal pattern of your life and consequently—inadvertently, perhaps—make trouble.

Motherpeace then is transformational because of this inherent disruption. In my experience, all the women who come to me for readings, healing consultations, bodywork sessions, or classes have the consequences of these issues foremost in their minds. Women searching for their real work, mothers wanting to find the courage to advocate for their children in the face of a dominating father, Catholic women who want to be priests, Buddhist women who want their meditative and spiritual experiences to be reflected in the lived life of the sangha (community), corporate women who deserve promotions they don't get, women musicians who can't get record deals unless they get a breast-job, and all the women whose voices and ideas are consistently erased, denied, overlooked, or trivialized in favor of male points of view.

Motherpeace is a worldview that is deliberately female centered in its philosophical perspective. When you use the Motherpeace cards (and certainly there are men as well as women who use them), you are entering a realm where you act "as if" women are equal and your point of view matters. It's not that men aren't depicted in the cards, it's just that the ways they are depicted is qualitatively different from cultural norms.

For example, the Emperor card in the traditional Tarot is considered to be a very positive character, and he is interpreted as being a king in a flattering and complimentary way. Traditional meanings always given for the Emperor alongside of this kingly glorification are "domination, war, aggression, militaristic power, the State," and so on. We didn't have to embellish on these traditional interpretations at all in making the Motherpeace Emperor; we simply shifted the perspective to a woman-identified one and let the image stand on its own. The result is that in the Motherpeace, the Emperor becomes a kind of indictment of all that's wrong with the world, namely war, domination, male aggression, and the militaristic violence of nation states.

The Motherpeace cards read reality through the lens of female equality and centrality, assuming these values to be positive, and they call into question practices that put women second or condone discrimination against women. Simply by virtue of providing positive images of women in various activities and roles, the Motherpeace cards rock the boat.

A woman in the privacy of her own altar can benefit enormously from using the Motherpeace cards, healing some of her own doubts and reassuring herself of her own worth. Used on a regular basis the cards become a foundation for centering and opening the intuitive awareness. But when a woman brings the cards out of the private sphere and into the public—in the neighborhood, at school or church, at her job, in community meetings, in her therapy sessions, with her children and her husband and her friends—it cannot help but create significant change.

AUTHORIZE YOURSELF

The first thing you need to do before you take the cards out into the world is to begin to self-authorize, to put yourself at the center of your own knowledge, which is where you belong. You need to become grounded enough in using the cards to know that they work, which means having enough hands-on experience with them such that they have proven to you that you can trust your reading of them and the guidance they have provided you so far.

So practice with the cards on your own for a year and a day, as suggested in earlier chapters, and learn the meanings of the images to your satisfaction. Become familiar with the process of doing a reading, then living your life, and returning to the reading later in order to corroborate your understanding of the cards in "real life." Trust yourself and test yourself until you know you can count on your intuitive powers of perception. When you have seen the cards hit the target a few times, and you have managed to "guess" correctly or solve problems effectively for yourself using them, then you will be grounded enough in your own use of the cards to begin to bring them out of the closet for use with other people who might be skeptical.

CREATE A POSITIVE PICTURE

It is important before taking the cards out in the world to assume or imagine that other people also (1) need oracular guidance, and (2) will respond in positive ways to the helpful hand provided by the cards. You have to overcome your own doubts and fears before you can use the cards successfully with other people. But you can begin by acting "as if" you completely trust the cards and you are very grounded in their use. This creative visualization will carry you a long way toward being the centered woman you are trying to become.

Detachment is the other thing you have to learn in order to be able to handle the unexpected moments in your episodes with the Motherpeace cards out in the world. You can't take other people's reactions personally. So detach yourself from any negativity that may be inadvertently catalyzed by the presence of the cards. You never know who is going to freak out, but *their* reaction isn't really *your* problem to fix.

You won't have much luck taking the cards out in the world if you get too serious about them or about yourself in relation to them. Keep it light. Make it playful. This breaks the ice for people. One of the most important things that can be accomplished through the use of the cards in groups and with people who wouldn't normally use them is the breaking of patterns in our belief systems. Consider that the cards act as a trickster and disrupt normal ways of thinking about things. Furthermore, they do so by speaking in a symbolic code that translates itself directly to the unconscious or inner mind, and in this way they bypass the much-too-rigid rational mind and go straight to the heart. Most of us are starving for more heart contact in our daily lives, so this effect—although not always comfortable—is generally appreciated. Remember the healing effect of laughter.

INTRODUCING MOTHERPEACE INTO UNUSUAL ENVIRONMENTS

You can take the Motherpeace cards anywhere you go in the world, and you can introduce them to anyone who seems open or interested in who you are or what you do. I have brought them out in settings where a more cautious person might not have done so, and generally speaking, the experiences have all been very successful and interesting. The cards add an unorthodox and creative element to whatever form or structure they come into. I've had amazing experiences with Motherpeace in other countries—especially, but not only, with women and children. If there is a language barrier, the cards can cut across it with ease, releasing tension and pulling people together around the concepts and ideas that live more deeply in us than conversation.

When I first traveled out of the country, I visited Mexico, traveling around with my new husband, exploring towns, cities, and ruins, and meeting the people who live there. My first really magical experience happened with three Mayan women at the ruins of Uxmal in the Yucatán peninsula, when I pulled out the Motherpeace cards and my English-Spanish dictionary. It was astonishing how much we were able to share on a philosophical level with the cards as the medium through which our communication took place. I had an amazing conversation about the Justice card with a Mayan grandmother who was an evangelical born-again Christian. We discussed fate and natural law, with me talking about *"la Diosa Terra"* (the Earth Goddess) and her exclaiming, *"No! Dios solamente!"* (only God). She excitedly described all the symbols in the image of the Norns under the Tree of Fate completely in biblical terms.

We bought huipils, embroidered blouses, from them, and then the older woman invited us to her house, *"la casa de Victoria Nobelo."* In shock, I told her that Vicki Noble was also my name. *"También!"* (Also!) she cried in amazement. I ended up doing hands-on healing for her husband, who was very ill, and they took us to a cave where there were natural stalagmites of an eagle and an owl. Later the family asked me and my husband to be the co-*madre* and co-*padre* of their first grandchild.

TAKING MOTHERPEACE TO WORK

Although it would seem that the American workplace would be the last area to assimilate the use of oracles and the intuitive female process, in fact I have known many women over the years who have successfully insinuated the cards into their work environments. One woman I know keeps them out on her desk at the biomedical corporation where she is an accountant, and within a short time of quietly introducing them into the environment, her coworkers were coming to her for readings. It all stays somewhat "under the table," yet at the same time she never hides what she is doing.

A simple way of introducing the cards into any environment where there are other people is simply to put them out, for your own use, but where they can be seen by other workers—on your desk, table, or any kind of work surface. You might get them out when you need to make a decision, simply using them in the ordinary ways that you would anyway, without hiding them. Don't be shy, but don't bring them to anyone's attention. Let those people who are naturally drawn to the cards come and ask you about them. Soon you'll be engaged in an organic process of bringing them into your working environment. People will undoubtedly begin asking for a card for the day, or even readings on difficult questions or decisions they are trying to make.

In a workplace where there are regular staff meetings or small groups of employees meeting for any kind of sharing, you might feel out the possibility of introducing the Motherpeace into the group process. Eventually they can be used for conflict resolution or just helping employees get to know one another better, but in the beginning it doesn't have to be anything more than just a card for anyone who's interested—very casual. Anytime people "circle" or gather together, they could be invited to begin the session by choosing a card for the day. Appeal to people's curiosity. Remember to make it fun, simple, and nonthreatening.

One thing I have noticed myself: women tend to be naturally curious and almost always say yes when asked if they want to choose a card. Men, on the other hand, can react in quite different ways. Recently when I brought the cards out after a formal dinner with people I didn't know very well, one man was outraged and responded, "Absolutely not!" But everyone else was totally enjoying the process, so I laughed and made a remark like, "Well then, that's clear," and simply went on with what I was doing. Soon the man who originally had been so threatened was telling us all about the artistic symbolism he saw in the cards, although he never chose a card as an oracle. Most men don't react so strongly, but they are quite often reluctant to expose themselves by choosing a card in front of all the others. Women generally lead the way in this kind of activity.

MOTHERPEACE IN THE FAMILY SETTING

Motherpeace works extremely well at home, bridging the communication problems that naturally arise between parents and children, or between partners. Because the cards are like a "third party" and neutral, nobody feels dominated by their presence, and everyone has an equal chance at being heard or seen for who they really are. General rule of thumb: it is less threatening for kids to describe a picture on one of the cards than it is for them to say directly what they want in a situation where there might be disagreement. The cards can cut through all kinds of conditioned responses, allowing people to be more authentic in a safe situation where they know they will be heard. It's therapeutic but disguised as fun.

When kids go through any kind of "initiation" or transition that ought to be recognized, the Motherpeace cards are a great gift, especially for girls and young women. But boys like them, too— they're just more affected by peer pressure to be cool and uninterested in such things. When girls first get their periods is an obvious time to present them with their own Motherpeace deck, or when kids graduate from middle or high school is another opportunity. Offer them a deck of cards when they have friends overnight; Motherpeace is the perfect slumber party entertainment.

Encourage your kids to develop their intuition, so that they will know how to make decisions that are not based on blindly going along with their friends. My daughters learned as young adolescents how important and effective it was for them to have a sense of their own "inner voice." Once when she was living with her father away from my home, my oldest daughter called me to tell me an experience she'd had the night before. It was homecoming, and there were two events planned for after the game—a bonfire at the school, and a kegger in the woods. I think normally she would have gone to the beer party, but that night her inner voice warned her to stay away, and she went to the bonfire instead. Everyone at the "woodsie" was arrested. She was very impressed that what I had taught her had so much practical merit.

OUT OF THE CLOSET AND INTO THE WORLD

Basically, there is nowhere you can't take the Motherpeace cards if you feel the impulse. The worst thing that might happen is that someone will react, and then you will practice your detachment and discreetly put the cards away. Most of the time, I think you'll be pleased at the way in which the cards open up possibilities that didn't actually exist through any other channel. They tend to make people relax and laugh at themselves and life, and quite often people feel touched by the intimacy that lies just below the surface banter. You may find yourself very popular as the "reader" of the images that have something to offer everyone who is curious enough to ask. It is characteristic of human nature that we like to see ourselves mirrored back in ways that expand our understanding and open our hearts.

Experiment with bringing the cards into settings where they would never be found on their own, such as the university, office, or school. I know therapists who use them regularly with their clients, and a woman once told me about the abbess of a convent who kept them on her desk in plain sight of anyone who came into her office.

Be aware of the pervasive gender gap that is happening all over America (if not the whole world) and can be seen in so many areas beyond traditional voter politics. What men are thinking about these days may not have anything to do with what women care about, and women's concerns might be quite surprising to men if they cared to investigate. The Motherpeace cards can be a tool to help you bond with other women like yourself, so that we create female solidarity in our communities and world. It has always been such solidarity that solved the problems we face collectively, and today it seems more important than ever.

Perhaps the most significant symbolic event of the 1990's was the meeting of women from around the world at the International Women's Conference in China in 1996. Like the 10 Discs with women coming together from different tribes—holding up their baskets with a variety of regional patterns depicted on them—each of us women has an opportunity at this time in history to give birth to a new aspect of ourselves, in a global circle of support.

No matter what our individual circumstances in real life, we belong—in the absolute sense—to a worldwide movement of solidarity among women of all races, classes, and nation-states. As the women from Palestine and Israel have demonstrated by joining hands across enemy lines, the mothers of the world want peace, and on that one overriding agenda—MOTHERPEACE—we are in agreement. So be it!

RESOURCE LIST

MUSICAL CDS AND TAPES FOR MEDITATION AND SPIRITUAL WORK

Jennifer Berezan, *She Carries Me* (with Olympia Dukakis).
Continuous twenty-six-minute chant to Tara/Quan Yin, plus instrumental piece; inspired Goddess liturgy, including reworking the Hail Mary.

Jennifer Berezan, *Voices on the Wind.*
On one side chants developed for use in Vicki Noble's healing circles; long continuous chant to Tibetan Tara on the other.

On Wings of Song and Robert Gass, *From the Goddess/O Great Spirit.*
Continuous trance-inducing choral weaving of three well-known Goddess chants by Z. Budapest, Adelle Getty, and Deena Metzger.

Rachel Bagby, *Full.*
Moving vocal expression of feeling and experience by this African-American singer/songwriter who tours with Bobby McFerrin.

Sharon Burch, *Yazzie Girl* and *Touch the Sweet Earth.*
Contemporary version of chants that express her personal view of the traditional Navaho (Diné) way of life in these inspired and beautiful recordings.

Ubaka Hill, *Shapeshifters.*
Inspired drumming and chanting from this African-American healer and teacher.

All of the above recordings can be purchased through: Ladyslipper Catalog of Music By Women, 3205 Hillsborough Road, Durham, NC 27715. www.ladyslipper.org
This is *the* resource for women's music of all kinds—a potpourri of the best of female vocalists, instrumentalists, performers, and choral groups.

This list is unavoidably brief and is designed as a starting point only. I recommend any of the many albums by Enya, Lisa Thiel, Mari Boine, Liz Story, Kay Gardner, Barbara Higbie, Loreena McKennit, and others. And in the World Music section of your local music store can be found tapes and CDs of Tibetan bells, Buddhist monks chanting, world drummers, etc.

The words and music to Bonnie Bramble's Hallowe'en song "Who Are the Witches?" were published in *SnakePower,* vol. 1, issue 1, Hallomas 1989, which can be ordered from Vicki Noble at P.O. Box 5544, Berkeley, CA 94705. Send $7.50 U.S. (includes postage and handling).

Charlie Murphy's Winter Solstice chant "Light Is Returning" can be found on the tape *Canticles of Light* (1984) from Out Front Music, P.O. Box 12188, Seattle, WA 98102. His much-loved song "The Burning Times" was performed by Jennifer Berezan on her first album, *In the Eye of the Storm,* which can be purchased through the Ladyslipper Catalogue.

MISCELLANEOUS RESOURCES

Lunar Calendars

The oldest and most established lunar calendar shows the changing face of the Moon as an oval shape, rather than the usual square calendar months. It's very helpful for women to begin to keep track of time through the visual use of such a calendar, since part of what we have lost over time is a sense of our unique lunar-menstrual rhythms. *The Lunar Calendar: Dedicated to the Goddess in Her Many Guises* can be found in most New Age, esoteric, or women's bookstores, and can be ordered directly from: LUNA PRESS, P.O. Box 15511, Kenmore Station, Boston, MA 02215-0009; 617-427-9846.

Astrological Calendars

If you are interested in keeping more precise track of the movement of the other planets in addition to the Moon through the zodiacal signs every month, you might like to purchase an astrological calendar that tells you every day what the planets are "doing" in relation to one another. When Pluto squares Venus, for instance, emotions might be intense, while a sun-Jupiter day might indicate more external or creative events.

The *We'Moon* calendar comes out of the experience of women living in Oregon country and incorporates a variety of women's art and graphics each year. (We'Moon at MotherTongue Inc., P.O. Box 1395V, Estacada, OR 97023 or E-mail: wemoon@teleport.com)

Jim Maynard's *Celestial Influences* ("almanac and textbook of astrology, ephemeris and calendar") and his smaller *Pocket Astrologer* are very helpful (one for home, one for travel). (Quicksilver Productions, P.O. Box 340, Ashland, OR 97520)

BUDDHIST CHANTS FOR RITUALS

For basic grounding in spirituality, I suggest using the Tibetan Sanskrit syllables "OM AH HUM" over and over, for as long as you
wish. These fundamental sounds open the higher centers in the
body, cleanse the aura of unwanted and intrusive energies, and create the supportive sense of an anchor or core at the center of your
being.

CHANT TO THE DIAMOND TEACHER (USING
MOTHERPEACE ACE OF SWORDS)

For deeper, more focused work, there is a chant from the Nyingma
school of Tibetan Buddhism that is understood to be an invocation
of the guru or inner teacher. The chant is technically dedicated to
Padma Sambhava, the male founder of Tibetan Buddhism, but I
prefer to use it with the Motherpeace Ace of Swords as a meditation device. With the card in front of you (a yogini in trance state,
enclosed in a diamond crystal, in a strenuous yoga posture) as a
visualization, chant the following three lines on three separate out
breaths:

OM AH HUM

VAJRA GURU

PADMA SIDDHI HUM.

When you perform this chant over a period of time, you are
invoking the higher powers, asking for help in forming what Buddhists call the "diamond body" or invincible body of light, and

praying for spiritual powers to build up in you. This will affect positively your immune system and your protective aura, grounding and centering you while helping you to focus on what really matters in your life and clearing the less important and distracting items from your mental space. I use this chant every day in a variety of ways—in my morning meditation while counting *mala* beads, when I go jogging, when I have trouble falling asleep at night.

TARA CHANT

The chant to Tibetan Tara is especially healing for women, as it invokes the Goddess who "hears the cries of the world" and responds. Tara is a Bodhisattva or world savior, a Buddha in female form whose vow to incarnate as a female through all her lifetimes is a model of divine self-love for women. A bodhisattva is a person (or Goddess) who chooses to defer personal liberation until all beings are free, and whose personal calling is to work in the world in response to the needs of sentient beings. When you chant to Tara, you ask the Divine Feminine to be present in your life, protect and support you, and to use you as an instrument for the well-being of others.

For visualization purposes, you might use the Motherpeace Star, Strength, or Judgment card while you slowly chant the Sanskrit syllables:

OM TARA TUTARE, TURE SO HA
OM TARA TUTARE, TURE SO HA

And if you want to listen to a tape of this chant, Jennifer Berezan has recorded it on one whole side of *Voices on the Wind,* which you can order from Ladyslipper Catalogue (above).

VICKI NOBLE'S COMPENDIUM
OF PRODUCTS

Training Programs in Motherpeace Tarot and Female Shamanism

"A year and a day" of study in Motherpeace Tarot on four separate weekends at a retreat center in northern California, and a "year and a day" of intensive work in female shamanism on four other weekends. Women only. For information and to register for either or both courses of study, write to the address given at the end of the appendix.

Cards and Books

Motherpeace Tarot Cards

The original round deck by Vicki Noble and Karen Vogel. Emphasis on women, healing, shamanism, multicultural world-Goddess religion. Insight into the shared language of the Women's Spirituality movement. Price: Regular size deck: $25; Minideck: $20

Motherpeace: A Way to the Goddess Through Myth, Art & Tarot

Vicki's original book to accompany the Motherpeace Cards, with a new cover and preface. Reissued. Archetypal descriptions with bold color plates, in-depth symbolism, and background. Celebrates women, multicultural world-Goddess tradition. Price: $17

The Motherpeace Tarot Playbook

A skillfully written, guided course book by Vicki Noble and Jonathan Tenney (contributed astrological section using MP cards). Explains methods Vicki teaches in her Tarot workshops; reversals, ways to play, esoteric systems. Endless hours of activity, explore inner knowing/archetypes, profound insights into structure of Tarot. Price: $21

Shakti Woman: Feeling Our Fire, Healing Our World (The New Female Shamanism)

Vicki's handbook, primer, and guide for contemporary women healers and women undergoing spiritual transformation. A "how-to" with politics. Beautifully illustrated. Price: $16. Out of print. (Available only through mail order at the address given at the end of the appendix.)

SnakePower: A Journal of Contemporary Female Shamanism

This publication came to a close in 1989, but back copies of the first two issues are still available. It was ahead of its time when in print, so most of the content is still timely. An interesting and educational read for women or anyone interested in kundalini energy and the regenerative, intuitive qualities of serpent power. Price: $7.50 incl. shipping and handling

Down Is Up for Aaron Eagle: A Mother's Spiritual Journal with Down Syndrome

"This bold, brave and beautiful book is a blessing to our time. Essential reading for all whose lives are touched by Down syndrome—and for the rest of us who want to come alive to our own wisdom and courage."— Joanna Macy, author of *World As Lover, World As Self*

Vicki shares her spiritual journey as the mother of a child with Down syndrome, a journey filled with brave and creative choices, life-affirming lessons, and a special kind of spiritual wisdom.

P.S. We are currently seeking funding to distribute *Down Is Up . . .* to organizations offering services for parents and children with disabilities. Let us know if you are interested in supporting us. Price: $12 (hardcover)

Tapes

Motherpeace Tarot

Vicki's teachings of Major and Minor Arcana based on the *Playbook*, including additional insights not in print. Send SASE for titles and information.

THANK YOU FOR YOUR INTEREST IN VICKI'S WORK.
BLESSED BE.
P.O. Box 1558, Freedom, CA 95019

NOTES

1. This reference and several following are quotes from Demetra George in a private lecture to our group traveling to Greece and Turkey in 1994. George's books about the Goddess in astrology are particularly helpful for women using the Motherpeace cards: *Astrology for Yourself* (with Douglas Bloch); *Asteroid Goddesses: The Mythology, Psychology and Astrology of the Reemerging Feminine;* and *Mysteries of the Dark Moon.*

2. For more information with photographs of the mummy, see "A Mummy Unearthed from the Pastures of Heaven," in *National Geographic,* October 1994.

3. By Western women I am referring to women of European background and not to African-American, Native American, Chicana, or other women of color with roots in non-Western tribal traditions. African-American women, for example, still speak in tongues as part of their contemporary Christian worship experience, and Native and Latin American women are often still in touch with "pagan" healing ceremonies and non-Western forms of divination. It is interesting to note that when the media divulged that Nancy Reagan had employed an astrologer, and more recently that Hillary Clinton hired Jean Houston as a psychic advisor to teach her hypnosis, a certain segment of the public was outraged over this governmental use of oracles, and the media had a heyday.

4. Charlotte King's *24-hour phone line:* 503-399-0139, *E-mail:* charking@viser.net, *website:* http://www.viser.net/~charking/ and *mailing address:* Charlotte King, 1273 Franklin NW, Salem, OR 97304-3901.

5. When a psychic awakening takes place, sometimes the energies aroused by the experience are hard to handle and require professional guidance. The Spiritual Emergency Network was started for the explicit purpose of helping people who are having frightening experiences with psychic or kundalini energies. Although the Network itself doesn't seem

to exist anymore (at least I was unable to find a telephone number), there is a resource book called *A Sourcebook for Helping People in Spiritual Emergency* by Emma Bragdon, published by Lightening Up Press, 885 N. San Antonio Rd., Suite R, Los Altos, CA 94022.

6. See *Summoning the Fates,* by Zsusana Budapest.

7. *Motherpeace: A Way to the Goddess through Myth, Art & Tarot; The Motherpeace Tarot Playbook,* by Vicki Noble and Jonathan Tenney; and the *Motherpeace Tarot Guidebook,* by Karen Vogel.

8. Some useful Women's Spirituality resources for rituals and prayers: *Motherwit: A Feminist Guide to Psychic Development* by Diane Mariechild; *The Heart of the Goddess* by Hallie Iglehart Austen; and any books by Diane Stein (from Reiki to *I Ching*) or Judith Gleason, whose specialty is African goddesses.

9. I have written extensively on these subjects of the snake, women, and menstruation as the basis for female shamanism. I published two issues of a magazine called *SnakePower* in 1989 and 1990; back issues can be purchased from me at P.O. Box 1558 Freedom, CA 95019. Also please see my book *Shakti Woman: Feeling Our Fire, Healing Our World (The New Female Shamanism)*.

10. In Great Britain the "Active Birth" movement has accomplished a great deal in this area. For information, books, and tapes, write to the Active Birth Centre, 25 Bickerton Road, London N19 5JT, England. Director Janet Balaskas has written several amazing books about active birth, including yoga for childbirth, which she teaches at the Centre; she is sometimes available to travel and teach. Her essay on the subject can be found in *Uncoiling the Snake,* an anthology I edited, published by Harper San Francisco in 1993 and now out of print. (But it can be found in libraries.)

11. One of the tapes I made to accompany the Motherpeace cards is a meditation through the chakras, in which you "pull psychic cords" that are causing difficulty and choose Motherpeace images to replace them. (See the appendix for information on ordering the Motherpeace tapes.)

12. See *Shakti Woman: Feeling Our Fire, Healing Our World (The New Female Shamanism)*.

13. *Motherpeace Tarot Playbook.*

14. The paper from which my talk was taken can be found in the journal published from the conference proceedings: *Mirrors of the Gods: Proceedings of a Symposium on the Huichol Indians,* edited by Susan Bernstein,

Museum Papers no. 25, 1989; San Diego Museum of Man, 1350 El Prado, Balboa Park, San Diego, CA 92101.

15. See appendix for more information about ordering Tibetan chants and tapes.

16. J. S. Morrison. "The Classical World" in *Oracles and Divination,* p. 100.

17. Demetra George. *Asteroid Goddesses.*

18. O. R. Gurney. "The Babylonians and Hittites" in *Oracles and Divination,* p. 165.

19. Lama Chime Radha, Rinpoche. "Tibet" in *Oracles and Divination,* p. 14.

20. R. B. Serjeant. "Islam" in *Oracles and Divination,* p. 216.

21. Hilda Ellis Davidson. "The Germanic World" in *Oracles and Divination,* p. 123.

22. Lama Chime Radha, Rinpoche, p. 24.

23. Tsultrim Allione's eclectic *dakini* retreats, held at Tara Mandala in Pogosa Springs, Colorado, are open to both women and men, practicing or nonpracticing Buddhists. Allione was recently initiated as a Devi by a visiting Tibetan holy woman in an ancient female lineage.

24. Lama Chime Radha, Rinpoche, p. 9.

25. Canyon Sam, personal communication, 1997.

26. Just to bring this whole discussion full circle, when I was in southern Russia recently, visiting the museums mentioned earlier, I was fascinated to see that many of the Amazon women (with their mirrors and arrows) were buried in what the four of us on the expedition came to refer to casually as the "dakini posture," with one leg straight and one bent at the knee, the exact position of the icons of the dakinis created by Tibetans for the meditation and contemplation practices that are a part of their religion. Since the Dzogchen form of Tibetan Buddhism, which includes the dakinis, probably came into Tibet from the direction of Central Asia and south of the Caucasus, these forms could have also followed this migration, which would indicate a definite relationship between these two cultures.

27. Starhawk, *The Spiral Dance: A Rebirth of the Ancient Religion of the Great Goddess,* and Diane Stein, *The Women's Spirituality Book.*

28. See the appendix for information about this tape and others you can order.

29. In the first issue of the now-defunct *SnakePower* magazine (Hallomas, '89), we published the words and music to Bonnie Bramble's song

"We Are the Witches." To order back issues of *SnakePower,* write P.O. Box 5544, Berkeley, CA 94705.

30. Donna Henes, Urban Shaman, c/o Mama Donna's Tea Garden, P.O. Box 380403, Exotic Brooklyn, NY 11238-0403; (718) 857-2247.

31. Dorothy MacLean, *To Hear the Angels Sing: An Oddysey of Co-Creation with the Devic Kingdom.* Also see American herbalist Pam Montgomery's new book about working with the Devas, *Partner Earth: A Spiritual Ecology.*

32. Jeffrey Moussaieff Masson and Susan McCarthy, *When Elephants Weep: The Emotional Lives of Animals.*

33. For information, write the Michigan Womyn's Music Festival, Box 7430, Berkeley, CA 94707; or call 510-652-5441.

34. Michael Dames. *The Silbury Treasure* and *The Avebury Cycle.*

BIBLIOGRAPHY

Achterberg, Jeanne. *Imagery in Healing: Shamanism and Modern Medicine.* Boston: New Science Library, Shambhala, 1985.

Adler, Margo. *Drawing Down the Moon.* New York: Viking Penguin, 1997.

Austen, Hallie Iglehart. *The Heart of the Goddess.* Berkeley: Wingbow Press, 1990.

Bernstein, Susan. ed. *Mirrors of the Gods: Proceedings of a Symposium on the Huichol Indians.* San Diego: Museum Papers no. 25, 1989; San Diego Museum of Man, 1350 El Prado, Balboa Park, San Diego, CA 92101.

Blacker, Carmen. *The Catalpa Bow: A Study of Shamanistic Practices in Japan.* London: Allen & Unwin, 1975.

Bradley, Marion Zimmer. *The Mists of Avalon.* New York: Ballantine Books, 1982.

Bragdon, Emma. *Helping People in Spiritual Emergency.* Los Altos, CA: Lightening Up Press, 1988.

Budapest, Zsusana. *Summoning the Fates: A Woman's Guide to Destiny.* New York: Crown Publishing Group, 1998.

Colburn, Thea. *Our Stolen Future.* New York: NAL-Dutton, 1997.

Dames, Michael. *The Avebury Cycle.* London: Thames and Hudson, 1977.

———. *The Silbury Treasure.* London: Thames and Hudson, 1976.

George, Demetra. *Asteroid Goddesses: The Mythology, Psychology and Astrology of the Reemerging Feminine.* San Diego, CA: ACS Publications, Inc., 1986.

———. *Mysteries of the Dark Moon: The Healing Power of the Dark Goddess.* San Francisco: HarperSanFrancisco, 1992.

George, Demetra, and Douglas Bloch. *Astrology for Yourself: A Workbook for Personal Transformation.* Oakland, CA: Wingbow Press, 1987.

Greer, Mary. *Tarot Constellations: Patterns of Personal Destiny.* North Hollywood: Newcastle Publications, 1987.

Halifax, Joan. *Shamanic Voices: A Survey of Visionary Narratives.* New York: Viking Penguin, 1991.

Kerenyi, Carl. *Dionysos: Archetypal Image of Indestructible Life.* Princeton, NJ: Princeton University Press, 1976.

Loewe, Michael and Carmen Blacker, eds. *Oracles and Divination.* Boulder, CO: Shambhala, 1981.

MacLean, Dorothy. *To Hear the Angels Sing: An Odyssey of Co-Creation with the Devic Kingdom.* Elgin, IL: Lorian Press, 1980.

Mander, Jerry. *In the Absence of the Sacred: The Failure of Technology & the Survival of the Indian Nations.* San Francisco: Sierra Club Books, 1991.

Mariechild, Diane. *Motherwit: A Feminist Guide to Psychic Development.* New York: The Crossing Press, 1981.

Masson, Jeffrey Moussaieff, and Susan McCarthy. *When Elephants Weep: The Emotional Lives of Animals.* New York: Delacorte Press, 1995.

Montgomery, Pam. *Partner Earth: A Spiritual Ecology.* New York: Inner Traditions, 1997.

Needham, Joseph. *Science and Civilization in China,* vol. 2. Cambridge, England: Cambridge University Press, 1969.

Noble, Vicki. *Motherpeace: A Way to the Goddess through Myth, Art & Tarot.* San Francisco: HarperSanFrancisco, 1983.

———. *Shakti Woman: Feeling Our Fire, Healing Our World (The New Female Shamanism).* HarperSanFrancisco, 1991.

Noble, Vicki, and Jonathan Tenney. *The Motherpeace Tarot Playbook.* Berkeley: Wingbow Press, 1987.

Robbins, John. *Diet for a New America.* Walpole, NH: Stillpoint Publishing, 1987.

Sjöö, Monica, and Barbara Mor. *The Great Cosmic Mother: Rediscovering the Religion of the Earth.* San Francisco: HarperSanFrancisco, 1987.

Starhawk. *The Spiral Dance: A Rebirth of the Ancient Religion of the Great Goddess.* San Francisco: HarperSanFrancisco, 1979.

Stein, Diane. *The Women's Spirituality Book.* St. Paul, MN: Llewellyn Publications, 1987.

Vogel, Karen. *The Motherpeace Tarot Guidebook.* Stamford, CT: U.S. Games Systems, Inc., 1997.

Weil, Andrew. *Spontaneous Healing: How to Discover and Enhance Your Body's Natural Ability to Maintain and Heal Itself.* New York: Fawcett, 1996.

INDEX

ABOUT THE AUTHOR

VICKI NOBLE, born in 1947 and raised in Iowa, awakened to the Goddess and Women's Spirituality on her arrival in Berkeley, California, in 1976. Through a "shamanic healing crisis," she opened psychically to the healing, art, yoga, and divination process that led to the creation of Motherpeace. Since then she has written several books, developed a powerful ritual healing process, taught and lectured internationally, and led tours of women on pilgrimage to sacred Goddess sites around the world.

Vicki has raised two daughters—Robyn and Brooke—and lives with her special son Aaron Eagle, who was the subject of her last book, *Down is Up for Aaron Eagle*. She teaches in the Women's Spirituality Programs at the California Institute of Integral Studies and the New College in San Francisco, sees private clients for astrology readings and healing sessions, and is working on the establishment of an ongoing training program for women in shamanic healing arts and Goddess spirituality.

BOOKS OF RELATED INTEREST

THE DOUBLE GODDESS
Women Sharing Power
by Vicki Noble

THE TRIPLE GODDESS TAROT
The Power of the Major Arcana,
Chakra Healing, and the Divine Feminine
by Isha Lerner

INNER CHILD CARDS
A Fairy-Tale Tarot
by Isha Lerner and Mark Lerner

THE GODDESS IN INDIA
The Five Faces of the Eternal Feminine
by Devdutt Pattanaik

LADY OF THE BEASTS
The Goddess and Her Sacred Animals
by Buffie Johnson

VIRGIN MOTHER CRONE
Myths and Mysteries of the Triple Goddess
by Donna Wilshire

GOSSIPS, GORGONS & CRONES
The Fates of the Earth
by Jane Caputi

THE GREAT GODDESS
Reverence of the Divine Feminine
from the Paleolithic to the Present
by Jean Markale

Inner Traditions • Bear & Company
P.O. Box 388
Rochester, VT 05767
1-800-246-8648
www.InnerTraditions.com

Or contact your local bookseller